Caio Marco Antonio

Once upon a time there was Islam

Youcanprint *Self-Publishing*

Titolo | Once upon a time there was Islam
Autore | Caio Marco Antonio

ISBN | 978-88-93068-94-9

Youcanprint Self-Publishing
Via Roma, 73 – 73039 Tricase (LE) – Italy
www.youcanprint.it
info@youcanprint.it
Facebook: facebook.com/youcanprint.it
Twitter: twitter.com/youcanprint.it

Thanks to your democratic laws we will invade you.
Thanks to our religious laws we will dominate you.

You sir, prefer your Allah who tells you to kill me in
order to assure yourself a place in Paradise, or
perhaps my Jesus who tells me to love you in order for
me to go to paradise, and so He would like for you to
be up there with me as well ?

This book that I have written was inspired by various e-mails sent to me by many people including some friends that live in some of the most disparate places on earth.

Letters sent via the internet by people who wanted to manifest their discomfort towards Islam and the illegal immigration by Muslims towards western countries such as our dear and old Europe, but not forgetting Australia, Canada and the United States of America.

It's obvious that European governments within the past twenty-years have not done much to confront and resolve this very important problem. Now is much more difficult to find a remedy for all the damage that has accumulated within these last years.. thanks to the congenital myopia of most of the political establishment in Western Europe.

Of course the 'do-gooders' which we have many in Europe, maybe too many, they have greatly contributed to worsening this phenomenon and now we find ourselves with this huge problem and with not an easy solution.

Every once in a while in the squares and parliaments of the various European capitals, the do-gooders defend the illegal immigrants and their rights. Let's not talk about our eventual duties towards them, immediately news crosses the borders of various nations, climbs the mountain ranges, crosses the seas and deserts, and it reaches where other poor people are awaiting to undergo the journey of hope, which in many cases it is a trip without return and without hope.

He who writes is not a man without a heart and not even selfish, but he is a man that sees things for what they are, but at least does everything possible to understand the facts and situations for what they are.

Going around the streets of Rome at night and seeing many human beings preparing themselves a "bed" for the night, using cardboard boxes in order to protect themselves from the pungent cold. it is not an edifying spectacle and it saddens me much seeing those human beings reduced to those terrible situations.

To sleep out in the streets during the summer months must not be very hard, but during the winter months the music changes, a lot, even if in Rome the climate is never too harsh.

Coming to Rome by train you can see scattered old couches with the usual cardboard boxes on the ground and some blankets in order to cover themselves from the pungent night cold. In Rome, the temperature at night can get as low as below zero.

You can begin noticing those mounts of covers, covering those poor miserable beings, trying to find shelter from the freezing cold, as soon as you reach Trastevere station, continuing to Ostiense station and onto Roma Tuscolana. Those without a roof, sleep on the sidewalks adjacent to the train stations, even near the tracks and under the shelters in order to take cover from the rain and also to have the sensation of having a roof over their heads.

It creates enormous sadness thinking of those human beings in this civilized Rome, forced to sleep at those bivouacs because they are resigned to themselves, without the minimum work that would permit them to have the appearance at a better life.

I was informed that there are young people volunteering to drive around at night with their car full of food and hot beverages to distribute to those miserable people, that at least besides putting something hot in their mouths they feel that there are people out there that are concerned for them without asking for anything in return, only within the spirit of altruism.

I believe those young people should be called the angels of the city or of the night, besides what they are called I believe they are without a doubt real Angels.

I was of the idea, and still am, that all the advanced countries should develop organic plans teaching those people in their country of origin how to cultivate their land using methods and equipment like the ones used in Europe, the United States and Canada, also to learn new professions that could be of help to their communities.

It should be our duty to supply those people with machinery and all other tools in order to work the land, and it should not be too difficult to send agronomists, mechanics, doctors, veterinarians, also whatever is needed to build small factories, those things should be foremost everything else.

I think that after an initial help and guidance they should become autonomous and independent.

To try and help those people in their country near their familiar affections, their friends their environment, should be the best solution for them but also for us.

In financial terms this method would cost us much less than all of the assistance that we are forced to give them, from the time that they are spotted at sea until the time they leave Italy to go to other European countries, or as it happens often they decide to remain in Italy, with all the problems that such a decision entails.

Besides the economic problems we have to add the social tensions and the inevitable frictions that arise between the Italian citizens and part of the immigrants.

There have already been those kinds of problems in the past and there are plenty of newspaper headlines that count for that.

It is obvious that it is not easy to live in those welcoming centers when they first arrive, for long periods without a clear future and the fear that they would be deported, and annulling their attempt to reach the much desired "Eldorado".

Let us not talk about the bigger issue, which is the constant loss of lives that are swallowed by the Mediterranean sea.

We haven't the faintest idea as to how many human beings have drowned and are at the bottom of sea within these last years, whenever a rubber dinghy with its load of human cargo of desperate women and children takes off the coast of North Africa.

It all takes place in a stealthy matter and no one takes note of their departure, not even the authorities from the origin of their departure, which naturally they say that they did not know. That rubber dinghy officially does not exist and if it reaches Lampedusa, Malta or even Pantelleria, it means that good or bad it has saved itself, otherwise it has sunk with its human cargo, and no one will ever know anything about it, besides maybe, the family and friends of the ones that had embarked on that dinghy with its final destination, the southern European coast. Not having any more news of their dear ones and their friends, would come to the conclusion that the trip of hope did not have a good ending.

We should ask the fishermen from Mazara del Vallo, Trapani, Pantelleria, Lampedusa and Agrigento if they have ever found remains of human beings stuck in their nets and if they find any still.I personally believe yes, but it is not publicized for obvious reasons, even if at times it has come to be known of remains of human beings stuck in the catch of fish.

The theme of my work is Islam and the problems that we have with a small part of this monotheistic religion followed by a great many people around the world. The Muslims occupy a large part of this earth and are scattered just about everywhere.

The majority occupy territories from the Atlantic ocean to the Pacific ocean, passed the Indian ocean to North Africa, the Middle East, the rich gulf states, Iraq, Iran, Pakistan, Bangladesh and the battered Afghanistan. Without forgetting Turkey and India, where more than 100 million followers of the Prophet live. We find Muslims in Albania, Bosnia and Herzegovina, Serbia and Macedonia, thanks to the Turkish occupation and the other countries that were part of the defunct Soviet empire, such as Kazakhstan, Tajikistan, Kyrgyzstan, Uzbekistan, Turkmenistan and many others still.

Many other African countries profess this religion, beginning with sub-Saharan countries, Somalia , Nigeria and Senegal, and let's not forget Indonesia, Java and Sumatra. To say that all those people have embraced the holy war, the jihad, would be a mistake, but to say that among those people lurk those that desire a holy war against Christians and Jews and anyone else that does not follow the precepts of the Koran, is a sacrosanct truth. Without a doubt there are countries that nourish terrorism and the holy war, my assertions are confirmed by reading the daily news reporting acts of terrorism deriving from Arab countries and or Muslim in general. Personally I don't care about religion or the color of the skin of the people that I deal with on daily basis, or the people that I interact with for various reasons.

What interests me is their behavior, their work ethics and the respect that they have for other people. My personal modest opinion is that the religion or the color of the skin of another person should not be a conditioning bias. In my life I have always used this yardstick with people in general and in all honesty I must say it has always been good for me.

I lived in Libya for many years during the 50's and 60's and I still maintain the friendships that I cultivated during that period.

I lived in Haiti for two-years and never had problems with anyone and Haiti is the first black, independent republic in the world. The population is composed mainly by about 95% blacks and the rest mulattos and whites, even as I was part of a small minority I never had any problems what so ever. This does not mean that I accept any abuse nor orders by anyone that does not have the right to do so.

The Islamic fundamentalists must understand that in Europe there are people ready to fight in order to protect their ideas and their liberty, and at the opportune moment they will know how to behave, even if the majority of the Europeans seem to be resigned and destined to be slaughtered.

Some centuries ago', most European countries did not intervene in a war that had become the liberation against the Turks and the very powerful Ottoman empire and left to fight alone the papal States, Genoa, Venice, Spain, the Knights of Malta and the Austrians which were successful in defeating the very powerful Ottoman fleet, thanks to the capacity and the bravery of the admirals, also the unquestioned valor and bravery of the commander of the holy League, the Austrian, Giovanni of Austria.

Even if inferior in number the Europeans inflicted a harsh lesson to Ali Mehemet Pascia' whom was forced to leave the Mediterranean sea and that practically saved Europe from a bloody occupation by the Ottoman empire.

Even on that occasion those European nations failed to intervene which at that time were very powerful. In particular I'm referring to Portugal, France, England, that with their fleets could have annihilated the Ottomans while imparting a severe lesson.

On the 7th of October, 1571, Europe was saved by a coalition. The holy League, which at Lepanto destroyed the powerful Turkish fleet, drastically reducing the Ottomans dreams of glory.

We need to keep in mind that until that time the Turks were going from victory to victory and no one had been able to stop this powerful and overwhelming war machine. They had been unbeatable whether by sea or land.

They even had arrived in Poland and Ukraine and were awaiting to beat and conquer the capital of the Habsburg Empire, Vienna.

A spontaneous reflection comes to mind.

Has anyone ever heard that the Buddhists ever made a dynamiter attempt, or the Jews, the Hindus, or the followers of Confucius?

Unfortunately I have to note that only the Islamists delight with those actions and this reflection I noted also to my Islamic friends which they could only agree with me.

I will change theme and instead I will prefer to talk about this very strange kinds of people called the do-gooders. They are a very dangerous kind that need to be controlled and we should make sure they do not cause any more harm.

Some people want to be good at all costs even when faced with such disturbing evidence and circumstances. They are the do-gooders and that is it, even at the cost of getting hurt by those that they persist defending with a vengeance. They are a dangerous breed and at the same time also stupid without making any logical sense.

Years ago', the do-gooders came out with such crap that only sick and obtuse minds like them could give birth to. They thought that it would be alright to change the very sign that accompanied our ambulances and all the hospitals and emergency centers in our country.

Those people were thinking to remove the sign of the Red Cross and replace it with another that would not strike the susceptibility of the Muslims.

The Red Cross is an integral part of our history and for more than 150-years it accompanies us whenever we have some sort of difficulty and or necessity.

You could find it right in the middle of two world wars on both sides of the barricades and well accepted by all contenders.

After all the bloody battles between the opposing parties, the field was left to the Red Cross until the doctors and the stretcher carriers would assist the wounded and alleviate the last breaths of the dying.

Those great minds proposed to remove this beautiful and glorious symbol in order to make the Muslims happy.

But the Muslims that came to Italy knew that this is a Christian country or maybe they were hoping to see minarets and half-moons instead of churches and crosses? Then after noticing this reality which they found themselves in, they could have easily made a return trip to where they came from to begin with.

The do-gooders say that not all Muslims are equal and that the majority differentiate themselves from the fundamentalist. I'm certain that this responds to the truth and we do not need the do-gooders to tell us. My Muslim friends and acquaintances are good people and do not accept the actions of the extremists and condemn them, just like we do. But they are part of a silent majority and are isolated by the rest of the Muslim multitude, which counts for several hundred-million followers, if they are part of a very silent majority that is to be verified.

In regards to this very point I would like to refer to an e-mail which specifically talks about a silent majority and a minority that are exceedingly troublemakers.

It is interesting to read what the psychiatrist Emanuel Tanya writes in regards to Nazism and of any other violent movement which is active at this time.

I think it is very illuminating and should put us on alert from the violent minorities, because in fact, being minorities are erroneously neglected and are tolerated as mere factions of bad behaving kids.

I will now tell you what doctor Tanya stated.

A man which family was part of the German aristocracy before the second world war, owned numerous properties and factories, answered in this matter to whom asked how many Germans in his opinion had been real committed, convinced, Nazis.

"Few Nazis were convinced followers of Hitler."

The Nazis in reality were few, but many were very happy of the return of the great German pride.

Even the few, would organize reunions all over the country, propagated their beliefs and their plans and began to intimidate the ethnic minorities. While trying to proselyte most and attacking verbally and factually those who did not share their way of thinking.

All this while the majority of the German people remained passive, considering them rowdy troublemakers. Many were too occupied with their businesses and their problems instead of giving importance to the rowdy troublemakers and the events that were to follow. So, the majority did not care at that time and in doing so permitted Nazism to gain control.

Before we realized what was happening they gained control of power, we on the other hand lost control of our liberties and our lives and that was the beginning of the end of our world as we knew it.

My family lost everything and I ended up in a concentration camp. The allies with their massive bombardments over Germany destroyed our factories and properties.

This is the explanation that the German citizen gave in regards to the Nazism phenomenon and his country.

A decisive minority, active, ferocious with a real bad soul that eventually has the best over the weak majority and unable to make strong decisions which surely would have saved it from the catastrophe that was to follow.

Everyday we listen to those thinking heads and the usual do-gooders, that tell us that Islam is a peaceful religion and of brotherhood and that the vast majority of the Muslims desires nothing more than peace and tranquility. That is all possible and true, but it is also true that in the end this will also be irrelevant.

This could be useful in calming ourselves a little bit and diminish the spectrum of fanaticism that is rampant and is infesting the world in the name of Islam. Hoping that it is a passing phenomenon and in a short amount of time it will all return to normality. The fact is that the fanatics affect the Muslim countries and in most of those countries they practically have freedom to act as they choose and to recruit.

It is the fanatics and the extremists that march armed to the teeth. It is always them that allow filming of the decapitation of the poor prisoners all in the name of Allah. It is always them that burn the poor prisoners alive, all in the name of Allah. It is always them that ferment religious wars against the crusaders and the Jews, beginning in the Middle East, Nigeria, Sudan and the Philippines.

How many know that in the Philippines the Muslims of Abu Sayyaf are trying to make of Mindanao an Islamic republic? It is a war that is been going on for years and there is no end in sight.

In the west unfortunately the situation has already degenerated but maybe we are still in time to save ourselves, but we have to take important decisions, drastic and unpopular, beginning in our own country.

It is useless to try and be good with those people.

Every concession made to them is considered as our duty and also a sign of weakness on our part.

Those people are driven by an immense hatred towards the west and all of its principles. They kill their prisoners without pity, in the most cruel manners, always imploring Allah, which I don't think is too happy with them and their actions.

They go to the mosques and preach hatred towards the Christians and the Jews.

They push their young ones to commit suicidal actions.

They kill homosexuals with no ifs and buts.

They would like to impose on us the Sharia.

They hate our women and consider them of easy virtue and prostitutes, instead their women are saints and immaculate, but on this subject I have my doubts, corroborated by my own personal experiences.

They dream of requiring women to wear the burqa, just to annul decades of struggle in order to arrive at a certain emancipation, to reduce them to simple objects.

Whenever the conditions permit it, they perform lethal acts in the western world, happy to have sent to the Creator a good number of infidels.

The problem in the Arab countries but even here in Europe is that the majority of moderate Muslims do not expose themselves in order to counter the others and I this way the fanatics and the fundamentalists have no obstacles, practically no opposition from those that should give it, exactly as it happened in Germany with the advent of Nazism.

Of the minorities that have gained power, history has many examples but evidently the politicians do not want to make treasure of the past evidence in front of their eyes.

Communist Russia was formed by a people that desired to live in peace without any blood spill, but despite that, communism in that large country was responsible for the death of about 20 million people.

The majority made of peaceful and silent citizens was totally irrelevant. Even the large Chinese population was peaceful, but the Chinese communists were able to physically eliminate about 70 million human beings.

The majority formed of pacifists and silent ones was again irrelevant.

The Japanese prior to the second world war were not exactly war-loving and everything else that it entails but in the end the Japanese killed about 12 million Chinese in the Far East, killed with swords, daggers and bayonets.

The majority formed of peaceful people and the silent ones was again irrelevant.

Who can forget Rwanda which basically became a slaughterhouse in the hands of the lawless minority of assassins which overtook the majority of the Rwandans made of peaceful and loving people.

The majority formed of pacifists and the silent ones was again irrelevant. History's lessons are simple and clear but we do not want to learn from them, so we leave events to take their course, even if that will surely destroy our world and that we believe in.

The Muslims that love peace and respect for others are at the moment irrelevant thanks to their prolonged silence and will be more so once the fundamentalists have conquered the reign of power.

The real democrats and lovers of peace, whether Germans, Japanese, Russians, Chinese, Rwandans, Palestinians, Somalians, Iraqis, Iranians and many more, all died because they did not counteract, speak out and take action against the lawless minority with its full intent on gaining power and impose on everyone their beliefs, while they were able to do so. Later it was too late and everything was lost, even freedom and human life. At the end their world came to an end.

The only countries that do not accept in a passive manor the attacks of the Islamic fundamentalists are Nigeria, Sudan and the Philippines. In Nigeria, the Christians and all others who do not follow the dictates of the Prophet, respond to the attacks with the same actions, so there are victims on both sides.

In this way, the Muslims from the north will repay them with the same token.

An eye for an eye, a tooth for a tooth.

All this might not be worthy of Christians and not follow the dictates of Christianity, but not everyone is ready to passively suffer abuse,

Attacks, death and destruction, from the ones that think they have the right to impose their ideas all over the world.

Evidently the Nigerian Christians don't see it the same way as the Muslim terrorists do, and to still have a little hope of salvation they defend themselves with their own arms and methods.

In Sudan there is a war that has been going on for many years between the Muslims and Christians, between North and South, so it is easy to imagine that some Arab countries are helping the fighters from the North in order to eliminate their adversaries from the South.

In the Philippines, with the Christian majority, there is a war being fought, even this one against the Muslims of Abu Sayyaf which occupy the eastern part of the island of Mindanao and the Sulu archipelago, which eventually would like to convert into an Islamic Republic.

I am naturally on the side of Nigeria, Sudan and the Philippines which are part of very few countries that are combatting the Sharia and the Islamic fundamentalist, unfortunately with their own same weapons.

The discussions and nice words with whom has knocked down the twin towers in New York, made large-scale attacks in Madrid and London and continued to carry out more attacks in numerous Arab countries, with the stated purpose to stop any attempt to peaceful solutions by the politicians, remain useless. Let's remember that those gentlemen continue plotting in the shadows and if they have not committed other attacks towards the western countries it is only because of their inability or thanks to the secret service from those western countries, one of which should be right in the foreground is the Italian secret service which has been able to thwart attacks and also apprehend components of terrorist cells tied to Al Qaeda.

The last such action took place in Bari, by the ROS Carabinieri, which in the region of Puglia have arrested components of a group of terrorists tied to Al Qaeda,

which was preparing to commit terroristic acts in Italy and the rest of Europe. Those heroes and paladins of Islam, besides all the other raving things, between their own communications and letters, referred to the Italians, Jews and Americans with derogatory names such as mongrels.

Honesty, I have my doubts to whom are the real mongrels, also because dogs are men's best friend, so what remains in this terminology is bastard, and we know who the bastards are.

With luck, the Carabinieri were able to apprehend them in time, interrupting their designed criminal plans.

Before I begin to transcribe all the other e-mails, I would like to refer to one of them, it refers to the speech given by the Russian president, Vladimir Putin, given at the Duma on April 4, 2013, in regards to tensions between the ethnic minorities in Russia.

"In Russia, Russian people live. Every minority, if it desires to live, work and eat in Russia, has to speak the Russian language and respect Russian laws. If someone prefers the Sharia law, we recommend to you to go live in those countries where that is the law of the state.

Russia does not have a need for minorities. The minorities have a need for Russia.

We will not guarantee those minorities special privileges and will not change our laws just to comply with their wishes, even if they will give loud protests yelling out discrimination.

We have to learn from America's and England, Holland and France's suicide, if we wish to survive as a nation. Customs and traditions of Russia, are not compatible with the lack of culture and primitive habits of many minorities.

When this honorable Parliament will introduce new laws, should think first and foremost at the interest of Russia, remembering that the minorities are not Russians."

The Parliament members of the Duma gave Vladimir Putin a standing ovation that lasted more than 5 minutes. I also applaud with all my heart.

Whoever desires to live in Italy, has to learn how to speak our language, briefly know our history, and foremost has to absolutely respect all of our laws, habits and customs.

If then there is someone that does not like our rules, should go back from where the hell they came from, just like what the Russian president Vladimir Putin was saying.

I have received another e-mail which refers to the speech made by the French Prime Minister which is not very different in substance, from the one made by Vladimir Putin.

For the first time, a French Minister has had the courage to say what he thought and also what a great many French citizens think.

Learn to live in harmony? Interesting attempts of rapprochement?

Help them at all costs in order to integrate? To show more solidarity and availability? Let' drop this nonsense.

To the Muslims that like to live under the Sharia law, was given a message recently, to leave France and search for other shores.

The government is monitoring those radical groups and fundamentalists in order to prevent eventual attacks within the country.

It seems like that Minister Francoise Fillon may have upset some French citizens that are Muslims, when he said that the immigrants should follow French law.

It seems to me that he said something very normal, shareable and so obvious that in other circumstances it would not have been necessary to stress it.

Take it or leave it.

Now I will refer to the speech that the French Minister gave which is very similar to Putin's.

"I am very tired of this Nation, where we worry continuously about not offending some individuals and their culture.

Our culture has developed through sorrow, suffering, burning defeats, and exciting victories by millions of women and men that yearned and dreamed freedom. Our official language is French and not Spanish, Chinese, Arabic, Japanese or any other language.

Therefore, if someone wants to live in France, be part of our society, has to by necessity learn our language.

The majority of the French population believes in God.

This is not a Christian obligation, or a political imposition. But it is also true that women and men have founded this Nation on the principles of Christianity, and this is clearly documented in our past and recent history.

Therefore it is appropriate and just to show the signs and symbols of our religion, on the walls of our schools and public buildings.

If God offends you, if our God offends you, then I suggest to you to go find another part of the world where to live, because God is an integral part of our culture.

We will accept your creed without any problems. What we ask of you is to accept ours, and to live in peace in harmony with us, in our home.

This is our country, our land and our lifestyle.

We are offering you the possibility to take benefit for everything, from past centuries, that we, the French, have won at the cost of great sacrifices and sufferance.

But if you are tired of our flag, our commitments, our Christian creed, and our lifestyle, we strongly encourage you to take advantage of another slice of French freedom, the right for anyone to leave our country.

If you are not happy here, then leave.

We will not stop you.
We did not force you to come here.
You are the ones that have asked to come here, so accept the country that you have freely chosen, just like we the French, found it and organized it.''
I must say that I would very much like that an Italian politician would make a similar speech, even if our situation differs from the French situation, at least for now.
I will now refer to e-mails recently received, this one in particular which has reference to the attacks on the 11th of September in New York.
It is said that the Arabic world condemns this terrible attack, but I'm not sure how true this is and so I reserve many doubts.
Most likely, those that travel constantly to western countries for either work reasons or scholastic, they do condemn it, but the vast majority with a culture that leaves a lot to be desired, without ever having left their country, I have many doubts that they condemn the attacks on the twin towers.
To conclude, I think that Islam is a problem for Europe and the rest of the western world.
Naturally this is my opinion which is shared by many citizens of this world.
The danger with our democracy is that it gives the right to vote to each citizen, ONE MAN ONE VOTE, and in about twenty-years if not before we will realize at our cost the huge problem that this law will have procured. Then it will be too late.
For all those that think that the problem does not exist or that it is an invented problem, when they will realize that it actually exists it will be too late for them to change their opinion and coming up with a solution.
They tell me that in Brussels, in Belgium, the Muslims administrate a district having won an election.

Every day shirts like this one are produced in great quantities, advertised and sold by either hawkers or at retail shops, all over the Middle East, literally by the thousands.

Which one of us would wear a shirt similar to this? Maybe an insane person. Not even an anti-American to the core, and in Italy we have many of those, would cross their mind to wear a shirt that basically praises the killing of 3000 innocent people that happened to be at their place of work, just like in all probability were doing every day.

I had the fortune to visit the twin towers by going to the many boutiques and other activities at the bottom of the towers,
to the top where you could see all of New York that extended down to the horizon.

At that moment the speaker was saying that there were 20.000 people within the complex.

While enjoying the view I had the sensation that I was on an airplane, probably because the building was swinging a bit because of the high winds, especially at that altitude.

It came to my mind many times that all those people that happened to be there on the day of the attacks, probably just visiting it just like I did in the late 80's.

Let's go to the next e-mail.

An Arabic student sends an e-mail to his father in Saudi Arabia.

Dear father, Berlin is a magnificent city, the people are very kind.

I like very much to live here, but father, I'm a little embarrassed whenever I go to the university with my Ferrari 599GTB plated in gold, while my colleagues and the professors come by train.

Everything else is OK. A hug, Nasser.

The following day Nasser receives an answer from his father.

My dear beloved son, I just transferred to your account twenty-million American dollars. Please, we do not like to be humiliated, you go buy a train yourself.

A hug, your father.

From the moment that the Islamic fundamentalists and the extremists wanted to force the burqa on the women, we will see what happened in Turkey many years ago'.

An important Turkish politician, which is considered the father of modern-day Turkey, devised a particular method and evidently very effective, in order to eliminate the burqa.

Issued a decree, to be effective immediately.

Of course this gentleman could have done it because he was a dictator, so the decree immediately found favor from the majority of the population.

This man was Mustafa Kamal, better known by his nickname, Ataturk.

The decree stated:

To be effective immediately, all Turkish women are free to wear the burqa as long as they desire to.
It should also be noted that all prostitutes are obligated to wear the burqa.
The following day not one Turkish woman was wearing the burqa. Not even the prostitutes.

The son of an illegal immigrant asks his father:
"Father what is democracy?"
"My son, democracy is when the Europeans work and we have all the benefits."
"But father, aren't the Europeans upset because of this?"
"Certainly they are upset, but this is called racism."

A young Arabic boy asks his father:
"What is this strange hat that you are wearing?"
The father answers:
"It is called a taqiya, because in the desert it protects the head from the scorching sun."
"And what is this funny outfit that you are wearing?"
"It is a djbellah, because in the desert it is very hot and it protects our body."
The son continues...
"And what are those ridiculous shoes that you are wearing?"
"They are babouches which help from burning your feet from the scorching desert sand."
The son asks again...
"Why do you wear this strange clothing if for the last eight years we have been living here in Vancouver and to our luck here we have no desert at least I have never seen it."

This particular e-mail denotes the mood of the English people towards the Pakistanis but all immigrants in general.
Nasser and Habib are two beggars that live in London, both have more or less the same "working hours". Habib takes home a maximum of 3 pounds, while Nasser come home with a suitcase full of 10 pound pieces.
Nasser owns a Mercedes, lives in a home without a mortgage loan to pay and has a lot of money to spend. Habib dreams of all this and so decides to speak with Nasser.
"I work exactly like you, the same time that you put in, how do you do it to bring home every night a suitcase full of 10 pound pieces when I at the most bring 3?"
Nasser tells Habib...
Let's see what your signboard says..?
Habib reads.

"I have no work, no wife and 6 kids to feed."
"Good." Says Nasser. "Now read my signboard."
"I need 30 more pounds to finally go back to Pakistan."

A couple of friends are playing soccer in their backyard, all of the sudden one of them tells the other: "I am proud to be black and a Muslim."
The other responds: "I think it's right, however I am also proud to be white and a Christian."
The other replies with anger: "You are a racist and a crusader."

From the moment that there are no more mosques in Venice, the government has authorized the Italian Muslims to pray for Osama Bin Laden on the streets of the lagoon city.
So far 543 have drowned

The changes to the Eiffel tower have been completed.

THE MUSLIMS ARE NOT HAPPY
The Muslims are not happy in Gaza.
The Muslims are not happy in Egypt.
The Muslims are not happy in Libya.
The Muslims are not happy in Iran.
The Muslims are not happy in Iraq.
The Muslims are not happy in Yemen.
The Muslims are not happy in Pakistan.
The Muslims are not happy in Syria.
The Muslims are not happy in Lebanon.
The Muslims are not happy Afghanistan.
The Muslims are not happy in Tunisia.
The Muslims are not happy in Algeria.
So, where are they happy?
The Muslims are happy in Australia.
The Muslims are happy in Belgium.
The Muslims are happy in Canada.
The Muslims are happy in Denmark.
The Muslims are happy in France.
The Muslims are happy in England.
The Muslims are happy in Italy.
The Muslims are happy in Norway.
The Muslims are happy in Portugal.
The Muslims are happy in Spain.
The Muslims are happy in Sweden.
The Muslims are happy in America.
The Muslims are happy in Austria.
The Muslims are happy in Holland.
The Muslims are happy in Ireland.
The Muslims are happy in Finland.
The Muslims are happy in Luxembourg.

The Muslims are happy in every country that it is not a Muslim country.

Who do they take it out on?

Not with their leadership and their politicians, not with Islam, not with themselves.

They take it out on those countries where they now live, happily and working.

The countries that do their absolute best to make them feel like they are in their country of origin, from where they escaped and were very unhappy.

Please tell me, is all this intelligent?

Frankly, I have my doubts.

WELCOME TO FRANCE

After you will see three photos of what happened on a public transportation bus, in Paris. There is also a video from which the following photos were taken.

It is incredible that a group of crazy men, all of the sudden decided to recite out loud verses of the Koran, face to face with other citizens which most likely were not Muslims. After all, they happened to be in a great capital of a great nation, France, and not in Cairo, Jeddah nor Bagdad, and certainly in this city there would still be around some Christians, Hebrew and Buddhist.

Had they done this at a park or a beach, it wouldn't have been that serious, grave, like it was very grave having done it on a public bus, with their shouts and rowdiness.

Luckily in Italy those acts have not happened yet, because my fellow citizens are less tolerant than the French and the northern Europeans in general. Also because the infiltration by the Muslim Arabs in general, without a doubt is less pronounced than in France and England. I think the bus driver in Rome, or in any other Italian city, would have told them to stop what they were doing and would have certainly called the Carabinieri, surely blocking the exit doors so they wouldn't get away.

Or probably, first he would have called the Carabinieri and then would have told them to stop what they were doing. For those of you that would like to see the video in its entirety of this arrogant act, you can see it on you tube, this is the link:

"LE RACISM EN COURSE" and "ISLAM EN FRANCE" on YouTube.

Three photos of their public display of their prayer and the shouts on the public transportation bus, in Paris.

JAPAN AND THE MUSLIMS
The Japanese are a very particular race and very admirable under many aspects.
Have you ever read in a newspaper or listened on the radio or watched on TV that a leader or a Prime Minister of an Arabic country had visited Japan?
Have you ever read that an Iranian Ayatollah, or a Prince or a Saudi king that ever visited the Land of the Rising Sun.
Japan is a county that keeps Islam at a distance.
Japan has imposed strict restrictions to the Muslims and Islam all together.
Frankly I am not too sure that all of which will be listed following this paragraph actually imposed in Japan, but this e-mail was sent to me as it is, I only limited myself in translating it. Here, following are the restrictions imposed by the Japanese towards the Muslims:
Japan is the only country that does not allow citizenship to the Muslims.
In Japan, it is not allowed for a Muslim to get a permanent residence.
There is a strict ban to propagate oneself to Islam.
At the universities, Arabic is not admissible. In Japan, you cannot import the Koran written in Arabic.
According to data published by the Japanese government, there was given a temporary residence to two Muslims, which must follow Japanese laws while in its territory. Learn the Japanese language, and only engage in their religious rituals inside their residences.

Japan, is one of a few countries to have very few embassies in the Islamic countries.

The Japanese population is not at all attracted by Islam.

The Muslims that reside in Japan are employed by foreign companies.

Up to now, not even doctors are guaranteed visas, nor engineers or Muslim managers.

Within the most important companies in the country, it is written in their rules and regulations that no Muslims can apply for a position there.

The Japanese government is of the opinion that the Muslims are fundamentalists, and even in the era of globalization they are not willing to change their laws in regards to the Muslims.

Muslims find it very difficult even to rent a house in Japan.

If someone comes to know that a tenant is Muslim, then all the neighbors are on alert.

No one can open a "Madrasa" in Japan.

In Japan, nowhere near is there any law in regards to the Sharia.

If a Japanese woman marries a Muslim, is considered lost forever.

According to Mr. Kumiko Yagi, professor of Arab-Islamic research at the university of Tokyo, the Japanese think that Islam is a very aggressive religion and need to stay afar.

The freelance journalist, Mohammed Juber, has travelled to many Islamic countries after the attacks on the twin towers in New York, and was also in Japan. He says that the Japanese have a conviction..

"The citizens of the Land of the Rising Sun, are more than sure that the extremists will never be able to commit such act in their country. If this were to be true, my esteem for Japan would increase many a times."

ARABS BOYCOTT JEWISH PRODUCTS

Sometime ago', at the United Nations, an ambassador from an Arab country, made a speech saying that time had come for all Arab countries to boycott all Jewish products or any product that had something to do with Jews or Israel.

In response to that speech, the Pharmacist Meyer M. Treinkman, decided to help the Arabs at this very difficult and complicated project, by giving them a list of pharmaceutical products which have a connection with the Jews and or Israel.

The list is long but it will be very helpful for the Arabs and the Muslims to activate their threat and their project.

Every Arab that is afflicted by syphilis should not get cured with Salvaran, which was discovered by the scientist Paul Ehrleh, winner of the Nobel in 1908, together with the Russian Ilya IlychMechnikov, for medicine and physiology, in recognition for their work on the immunity system. Ehrleh, of course, was Jewish. An Arab that wants to follow the advice of the ambassador should not even take the Wasserman Test, in order to discover whether he has syphilis or not, because this test was discovered by a Jew, doctor August Paul Von Wasserman, died in Berlin on the 16th of March, 1925.

If an Arab or a Muslim suspect to have contracted Gonorrhea, he should not do the diagnosis, because in this case he would have to use a method invented by the Jewish doctor, Neissner.

An Arab that has cardiovascular problems, should not use the Digitalis, discovered by Ludwig Traube, because unfortunately for them he also happens to be Jewish.

If then they suffer of toothaches, should not use Cocaine, discovered by Widal and Weil, Jewish of course. If an Arab has Diabetes, should not use Insulin, discovered from the research of Minkowsky, once again, Jewish.

If an Arab suffer with headaches, should not use Pyramidon and Antipyrine, due to the research done by Spiro and Ellege, they were also Jewish.

Arabs that are afflicted by convulsions, should abandon the use of Chloral Hydrate, because that has something to do with the Jewish doctor, Oscar Leibreich.

Arabs with mental problems, or physical, should avoid following the thinking and cures of Sigmund Freud, father of the psychoanalysis, even he was a Jew.

An Arab boy afflicted with diphtheria, according to the Arab ambassador at the United Nations, should stay away from the Schick test, which was invented by the Jewish doctor, Bela Schick.

The Arabs should not be treated with methods invented Nobel winner, doctor Robert Baram, for ear conditions and also brain. He too was Jewish.

Arab kids would die and or remain crippled for the rest of their lives, if they were not given an anti-polio vaccine, discovered by Jonas Salk. He was Jewish.

Arabs should refuse to use Streptomycin, and continue to die from tuberculosis, because doctor Zalman Waxman, which invented this prodigious medicine in order to combat this lethal illness. He as well, was Jewish. The Arab doctors should not prescribe any medicines that have anything to do with the doctors, scientists and researchers that happen to be Jewish. But I'm In the opinion that they will not do it in order not to endanger the lives of their patients. I forgot to tell you about the findings and subsequent improvements on the subject, by dermatologist Judas Sehen Benedict and the findings by lung specialist, Frawnkel that together with all the other Jewish scientists, have combatted these diseases and all the problems caused by it.

Many people were saved by medicines discovered by Jewish researchers and Jewish doctors, which have studied and worked in order to alleviate the suffering and pain that afflict all humans, without discriminating against nationality, race and or religion. That means that also the Arabs gained from it.
These Jewish scientists, like all other scientists form other ethnic backgrounds, have all worked and studied in order to alleviate the pain and suffering that afflict humanity, of course the Arabs and Muslims are an integral part of the human race.

This e-mail talks about a rich Arab sheikh, and a Scottish man.
An Arab sheikh was hospitalized for an operation on his heart, but prior to the operation the doctors decided to have an extra supply of blood in case they had necessity. When they found out that the patient had a very rare blood type, they had to make an international request. Later they found a Scottish donor, fortunately with the same blood type as the sheikh. The Scottish man was very happy to have been able to donate his blood to the Arab man. After the operation, in order to repay, or compensate the Scottish man for what he had done, sent him a brand new BMW, diamonds and also a small fortune in cash.
Some months after, the sheikh had to undergo another corrective surgery, so the doctor called once again the Scottish donor, which was very happy to donate his blood once again to the sheikh, thinking of what he had received in return the first time.
After the second surgery, the sheikh sent the donor a letter of gratitude with a small box of chocolates.
The Scottish man was astonished by this act, thinking that the sheikh would have repeated the same acts as before.

So he called the sheikh and told him that he was surprised that
he had not received a gift of a certain value, just like the first
time.
The Arab answered:
"My dear benefactor, I also have Scottish blood flowing in my
veins."

THE ARAB AND THE GENIE

An Arab has spent many days crossing the Sahara desert, without ever finding a drop of water. He was in real bad conditions, even his camel was dying of thirst.

He was dragging himself on the sand and was thinking to be in his last moments of life, when he spotted an object covered by the sand and shining with the sunlight.

He got closes to the object and took it out of the sand and saw that it was a bottle of wine of Manischewitz. He figured that maybe there was a drop of wine left for him to drink, so he pulled the cork and a genie came out. This genie looked like an ultra- religious Hasidic Rabbi. He had a black outfit and a black hat. The braids that came down from under his hat. All the elements that are distinguishable to an ultra- religious rabbi.

"My dear man, you know how these things work, you have at your disposal three wishes."

"I will never trust you." The Arab replied. "I will never trust a Jewish genie."

"What do you have to lose, you have arrived at the end, you are dying and you don't realize it." The genie replied.

The Arab thought about those word and came to the conclusion that in effect the genie was right.

"Alright, I would like be in a lush oasis, with a lot of food and drinks."

"Very well, now I would like to know your second wish."

"I would like to be rich beyond any imagination." The Arab answered.

All of the sudden he found himself surrounded by baskets full of precious rocks, priceless old coins, necklaces and bracelets, a real treasure.

"OK man, you still have one last wish and make sure it is a good one." The genie said.

After thinking a bit, the Arab answered.

"I would like, that no matter I will find myself, that beautiful women will want me and desire me."

All of the sudden he was transformed into a tampon.

The moral of this story is that if an Arab does business with a Jewish genie, in the end there is always a rip off.

SOLCIAL SECURITY

Pensions and benefits for the assisted, in England.
Following will be shown all that is beneficial to the assisted people.
FANTASTIC, NEW, FROM SOCIAL SECURITY IN THE UK CONCERNING PENSIONS AND BENEFITS.

نور اگر رفت سایه پیدا نیستنقش دیوار و چشم خیره
ر رفت .ما نقش سایهدگر نمي دان نور اگر رفت سایه
نور اگر رفت سایه پیدا نیست نقشدیوار و چشم خیره ما نقش سایهدگر نمي دان
ر رفت دیوار و چشم خیره ما نقش سایه دگر نمي دان نور اگر .نور اگر رفت سایه
رفت سایه پیدانیست نقش دیوار و چشم خیره ماسایه
دیوار و چشم خیره ما نقش سایه دگر نمي دان نور اگر رفت سایه پیدانیست نقش
دیوار و چشم خیره ماپیدا
نیست نقش

If I hear anything else, I'll let you know

LITTLE BRUCE

We are in Melbourne, Australia.
Mohammed enters in the classroom.
"What is your name?" Asks the teacher.
"Mohammed." Answers the boy.
"We are in Australia, and we don't use names like Mohammed.
From now on your name will be Bruce." The teacher tells him.
In the afternoon Mohammed returns home.
"How was your day Mohammed?" The mother asks.
"My name is no longer Mohammed. I am in Australia and my name is Bruce."
The boy answers.

"Are you embarrassed by your name? Are you trying to dishonor your parents? Your past, your religion? You should be ashamed." She gives him a beating,
Then the mother calls the father and explains to him what has just happened. At that point even the father gives him a serious beating. The following day, Mohammed returns to school.
As soon as the teacher notices the bruises on the boy's face, she asks him what has happened.
"Yes teacher, two hours after becoming Australian I was attacked by two Arab terrorists."

SIMPLY INDESCRIBABLE

In Iran, an 8-year old boy was taken away for stealing bread at a grocery store.
The punishment for this offense was very harsh.
A heavy vehicle passes over the boy's arm, breaking it in many pieces.
The arm will be lost forever and the boy will never be able to use it again.
This was happening in the Muslim Iran, with Mr. Ahmadinejad in power.

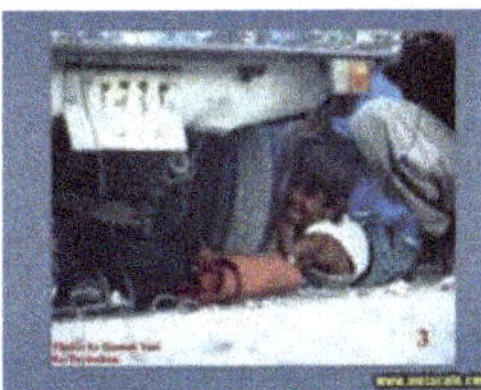
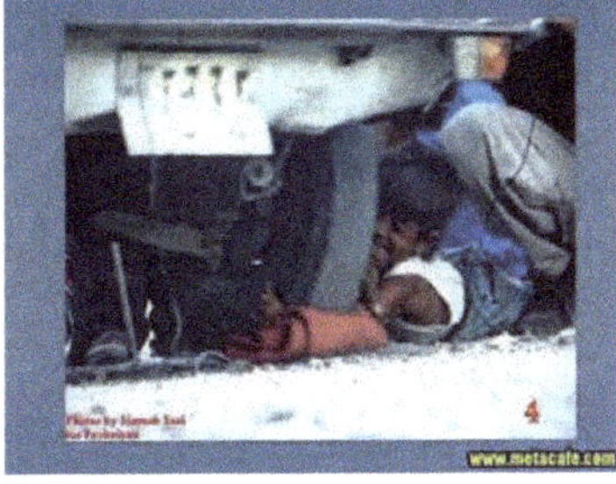
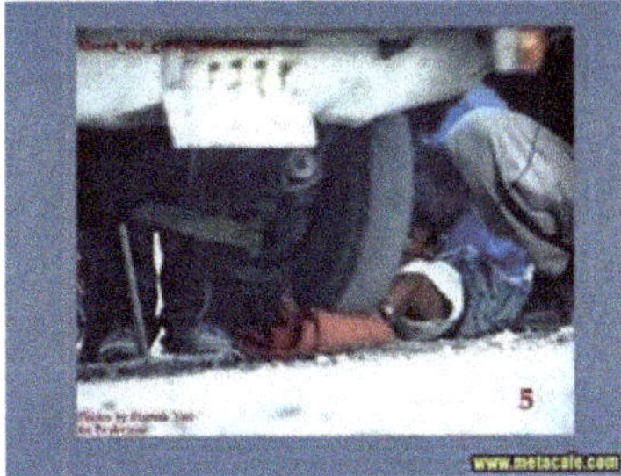

IF YOU WOULD LIKE TO GO THROUGH SOMETHING VERY BAD AND DIE A VIOLENT DEATH, TRY AND DO ONE OF THESE THINGS IN A MUSLIM COUNTRY.

a.   Go to Pakistan, Iraq, Iran, illegally. Don't worry about entry visa, immigration laws or anything like that. Just ask for the state to give you a home, food and other benefits.

b.   Once you are in one of those countries, ask the local government for free medical care, for yourself and the rest of your family. Naturally, without paying a cent.

c.   Insist that the doctors and nurses speak your language fluently, and all the food that will be given to you must be cooked according your specifications.

d.   Ask that the government documents and all official paperwork, be translated in your language of birth.

e.   Procreate, possibly a child every two-years and keep in mind that only a brief contact is needed to impregnate your wife.

f.   Maintain your national identity with determination. Place your country's flag on the balcony where you live, or a window. Place one on your bumper as well.

g.   Anywhere you go speak your language, at home and in public, and make sure that also your kids do the same.

h.   At school, ask for special classes just for you, in your language, where you can study the culture from your home country as if you were in a Muslim schooling system.

i.   Ask for a local driver's license, based on your original driver's license and original insurance from your country.

j.   This will bring you other legal rights and it will legalize your presence in Pakistan, Afghanistan, Iraq and Iran.

k.   Drive without having paid the automobile tax and insurance and ignore the traffic laws.

l.   Insist that the police speak your language.
m.   Organize marches of protest against your host country, enticing violence against none-whites and none-Christians and the government that let you in the country.
Good luck.

While these things happen in the west on daily basis, if you do the same in a Muslim country you will end up dead without a doubt.
Only in most European countries and in Australia, Canada and the United States, is what you have read permitted to all aliens, whether legal or not.

Unfortunately we are guided by people that care only about one thing, to be "politically correct". Weak, fearful to offend anyone, even those that come to demand for privileges in our home.

Comment written by a British citizen after the riots and manifestations in London.

THE ONE WHO FED THE BIRDS

I bought a small bird feeder and hung it on the ceiling of my patio, so I filled it with seeds. It was really a beautiful manger. In less than a week there were about 100 birds, feeding on seeds, which were there in abundance for them. For free. But then the birds began building nests along the edges of the patio, on the table and near the barbecue. Then of course, the excrements begin to appear. They were everywhere around the patio, on the table, the floor, the barbecue area.

Then some birds became intrusive and behaving bad. They were attacking me with their beaks at me. All this even after I had fed them with my own money.

Other birds remained on the bird feeder, chirping while emitting unpleasant sounds. At all times of the day and night they were demanding more seeds.

After a while I could no longer seat in my house, the backyard.

Then I decided to take away the manger and after three days all the birds were gone.

I then cleaned my house completely and everything became as it was before, calm and tranquil. No one was taking anything from me for free any longer.

Frankly, I now think that time has arrived for our government to take away this gigantic bird feeder so that most of these birds can take flight, or at least go back where they came from.

SCOTTISH DIPLOMACY

One thing that we have to admit about Scottish people is that their hearts and ideals are always in the right place.

Jimmy Mac Donald, an assessor in the city of Glasgow, was asked during a live radiocast, what he thought of rumors that suspects of terrorism were being tortured.

His answer won him immediate expulsion from the studio where the live radiocast was taking place, but an enormous applause by the public.

If what I'm about to tell you helps save even one Scottish soldier's life, then it's all good.

His answer was, "I would attach his testicles to an automobile's battery and would not say much, only red is positive, black is negative, and I would make sure that his testicles were wet."

THOUGHTS ON MUSLIMS

If you refine heroin for a living but you have a moral objection in regards to alcohol, then you are a Muslim.
If you own a machine gun worth about 4,000 euros and a missile launcher worth about 7,000 euros, but you cannot afford to buy a pair of shoes, then you are a Muslim fundamentalist.
If you have more wives than teeth in your mouth, then there is a good probability that you are a Muslim.
If you clean your rifle with your bare hands and consider bacon dirty, then you could be a Muslim fundamentalist.
If you think that clothing should be made in two styles, one bulletproof, the other for suicide bombers, then you could be a Muslim, potential suicide bomber.
If you don't remember anyone for which you have not declared Jihad, then you must be a Muslim fundamentalist.
If you were amazed in finding out that cellular telephones have other uses besides activating bombs on the streets, then you must be a Muslim bomber.

If you have nothing against women and you think that every man should have at least four, even if you cannot support them or give them pleasure, then you could be a Muslim doc.
If you find that what I have written above offensive and racist, then even you in all probability are a Muslim, or a do-gooder.

TERRORISM SCHOOL IN AFGHANISTAN

Course for bombers

Pay attention I am only going to show you this once

A POWERFUL EARTHQUAKE HITS THE MIDDLE EAST

A very powerful earthquake of 8.1 Richter scale hits the middle east.
Two-million Muslims are dead, over a million are wounded.
Iran and Iraq are completely destroyed, the governments do not know how and were not ready for such an event, in order to bring first-aid help to the victims.
The rest of the world is under shock.
The United States sends troops, mobile hospitals, doctors and food.
Saudi Arabia sends gasoline and diesel.

The South American nations send food.
New Zealand sends sheep, food and camping tents.
The Asian countries send workers in order to help with reconstruction.
Canada sends medical teams and food.
Great Britain sends two-million Muslims in order to replace the ones that have died.

OSAMA BIN LADEN IN HELL

Osama Bin Laden, once dead, goes immediately to hell, where the devil is waiting for him impatiently, in order to assign to him his due place.
"I really don't know what to do, you are on my list. But at the moment I don't have a place for you, but you must stay here anyway, I will have to find a spot for you. I'll tell you what I will do, I have a couple of people that while alive were not exactly bad, or as bad as you were.
I will let one go and you will take his place.
I will let you decide which one should go."
Osama thought that the devil's decision was good enough and so he let the devil open the first door.
In this room, there was Stalin, which would continuously immerse himself in a pool but would come back up with empty hands. This was done, hour after hour, day after day, month after month, and so on and so on. This was his punishment in hell.
"No, said Obama, first of all, I am not a good swimmer, and I really don't know if I could do this every day forever.
So the devil showed him another room.

Here we saw Hitler, which was breaking stones, brought to him by other residents, using a hammer. The more he broke the more they brought, day after day.

"No, not even this punishment will do, because of my bad health. I have constant pain on my back, and this continuous movement would be a real agony, I would have to do it day after day, I cannot do it."

The devil, had decided to open the final door. Osama saw Bill Clinton, lying on a bed, with his arms tied and legs spread open. Bending on top of him was a beautiful woman, doing what probably was the best thing that she was doing while alive.

Osama then said to the devil. "Yes, I think that this punishment would be appropriate because of my health issues. I think I can do it."

The devil smiled and said. "OK Linda, you are free to go. We have found your substitute."

MUSLIMS IN TEXAS AND THE PIG FARM A Muslim buys about 6 acres of land, in Texas, near a pig farm. It was a family farm, in Houston, Texas. Now these Muslims are asking the farm owners to leave the area. This request was so absurd that the farm owner decided to organize pig races on his land, during Friday's prayers. What's absurd about this situation is that the new arrival tells whoever has been there forever, to go and leave the area. This is like the story of the wolf and the sheep, while drinking water along the river. The wolf was upstream and told the sheep that she was dirtying his water. I don't think that the Texan is a sheep. I ask myself a simple question, before the Muslim bought the property, in order to build a mosque, a cultural center for the Muslims, didn't he see that there was a large pig farm, an animal that they absolute refuse to have nearby and are disgusted by it?

Had he not noticed the farm, nor the smell? He did not think to ask someone as to what was in that farm and what the smell was?

In my modest opinion, the Muslim knew exactly what that farm was, he went ahead and bought the land in order to build his mosque anyway. He thought that eventually he would be able to get rid of the farmer and forcing him to leave, counting on the help of the do-gooders, that even in America are not few, especially the politically correct ones, but from the politically correct people I think the farmer does not care at all, and justly so if I may add.

If you wish to see the video, here is the link:
http://www.youtube.com/embed/dUr1NxJDC94?rel=0http://www.

VISITORS AT THE OSAMA BIN LADEN'S GRAVE

MUSLIM WOMAN OF THE YEAR

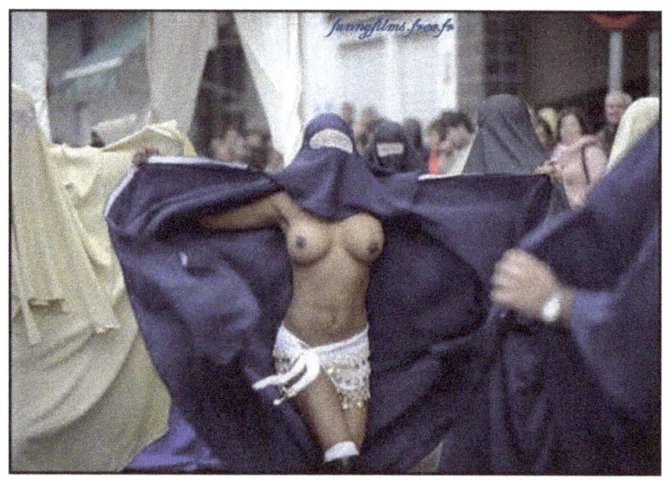

BURQA FOR AUTOMOBILES

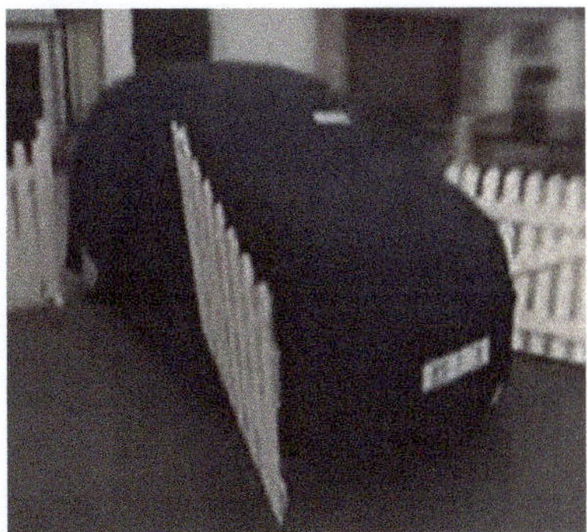

NEW STYLE BURQA

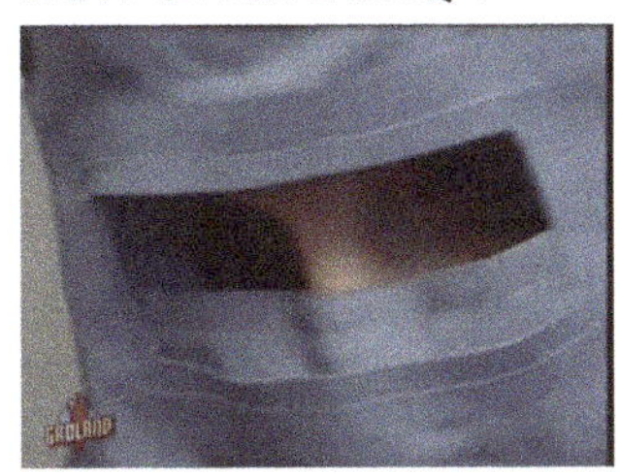
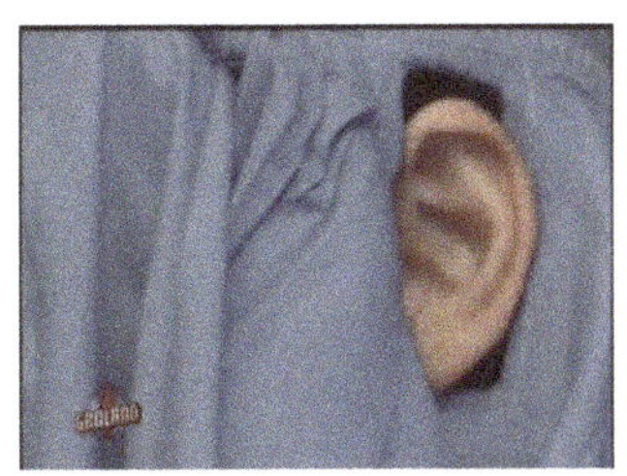

AT THE OPHTHALMOLOGISTAT THE OTOLARYNGOLOGIST

AT THE DENTIST

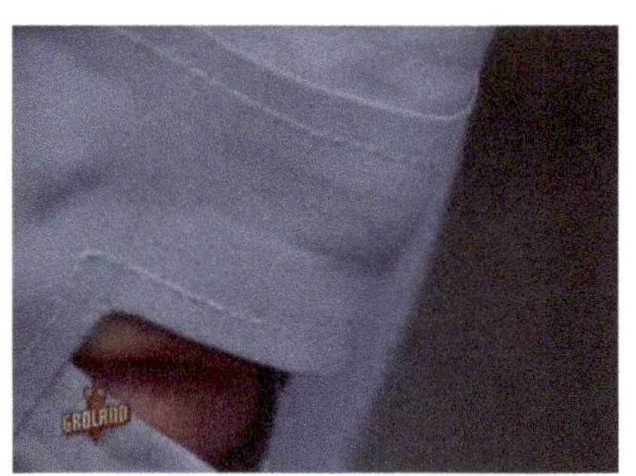

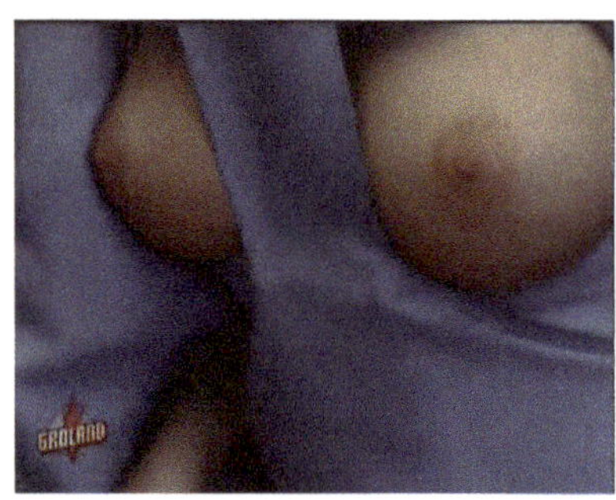

MAMMALOGY

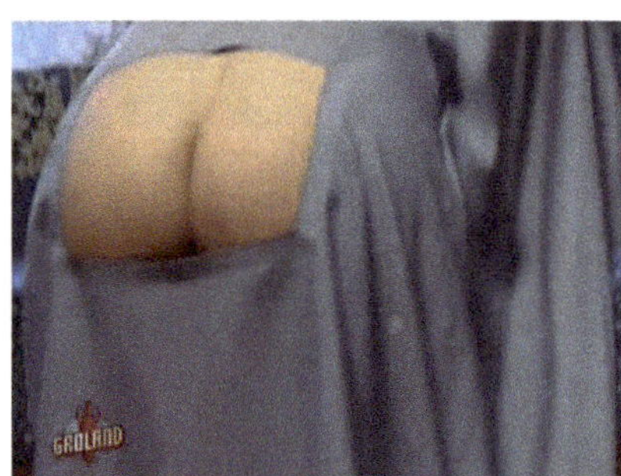

GASTROENTEROLOGIST

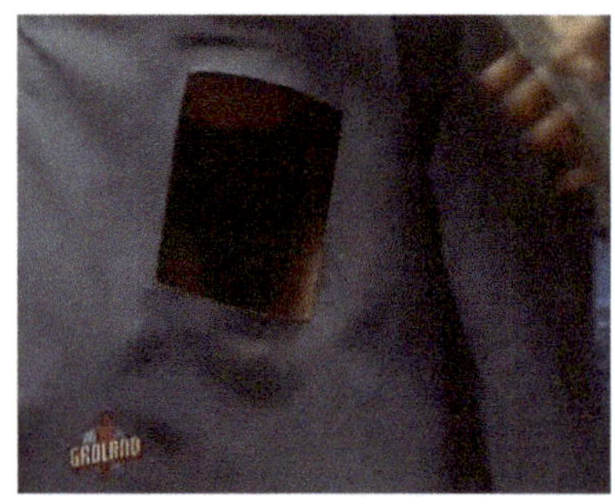

AT THE GYNAECOLOGIST

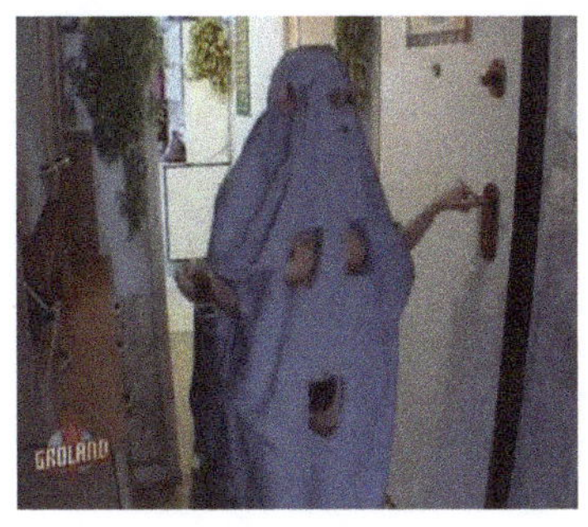 

A LITTLE COMPLICATED TO LEAVE THE HOUSE BUT IT CAN BE DONE

This e-mail is entitled ''3 BEAUTIFUL CHILDREN''

A GENTLEMAN COMPLIMENTS A MOTHER ON HER THREE KIDS.
THE WOMAN SENDS HIM TO HELL, RESENTFUL.
LOOKING AT THE PICTURE, I THINK THE WOMAN IS RIGHT,
THERE IS ONLY ONE CHILD, THE REST IS TRASH.

A GOOD METHOD IN ARRESTING A TERRORIST.

This incident happened in Spain.   Apparently Spanish police let a terrorist get away in order to calm his rage and situation with the hostages inside the bank. Police permitted him to exit the bank with a couple of hostages, got him a motorcycle, permitted him to reach it after letting go of the hostages. At this point the terrorist was permitted to escape on a street that had been cleared of traffic in order to facilitate this. As soon as the terrorist took off on the motorcycle, a police car suddenly appeared from a side street and made full impact with the terrorist, which flies off the bike and is eventually arrested. I don't know in what condition the terrorist is in but this is secondary to the fact that he was captured.

If something like this had happened in the United States, Canada, Australia, France, Belgium, Holland or Great Britain, most probably the policemen would have been seriously fined and suspended by the department.
The terrorist would have had a new bike and a check for 500.000.00 euros as compensation for physical damage. He would have received apologies by the Prime Minister and or the President. His family would have been invited, at our expense, to come to the country where he was They would have been given a house. We have to respect the terrorist human rights.

THIS E-MAIL IS TITLED BOOOOOOM.

How not to place a bomb on the side of a street.
Rule number 1.
After having placed the bomb in a hole, it is seriously advised not to press too hard on the dirt after covering the hole.
Rule number 2.
Absolutely never forget rule number 1. Otherwise...Boooooom.
The pictures that you see were taken with the camera attached to an AC130 machinegun, from about 1600 meters.

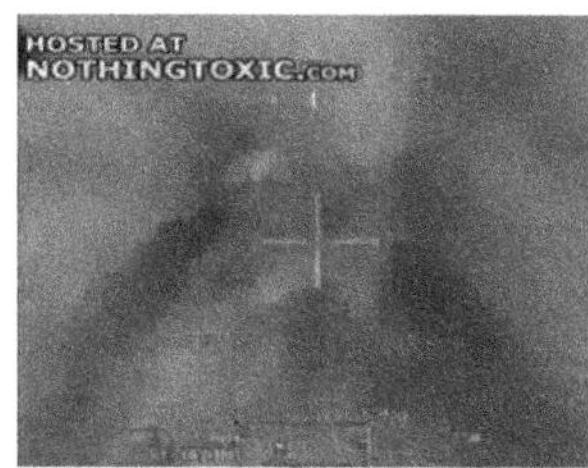

No shots were taken by the AC130 nor from planes nearby.

Some Islamic Jihadists were trying to place a bomb on the side of a street.

Evidently they must have lost the instructions booklet or did not know how to read it.

The problem was resolved by itself, without any intervention by the Americans or other coalition forces.

The Jihadists did it all on their own, and they were real good and efficient.

They acted on their own...and blew up in the air.

TOLLERANCE BY THE AUSTRALIANS

I'm really perplexed as to why many of my friends are against the idea of a new mosque in Sydney, Australia. I think it would show a lot of tolerance by the Australian if they would permit the Muslims to build another mosque in Sydney. So in my opinion the mosque should be built.

Always in the name of tolerance I ask myself, it should be allowed for nightclubs to be opened nearby.

Always in the name of tolerance there should be allowed a butcher's shop that specializes in pork, to open nearby and also a barbecue restaurant that serves pork meat.

Not too far away, they should also open a lingerie boutique, with a display window full of the latest sexy outfits.

All this would ask of the Muslims all that tolerance that they ask of us, in our home country, and of course the problem to build a new mosque would be completely resolved.

For all those that were offended by some American marines urinating on two dead Taliban men, I ask them to find out who were those two brave fighters that received this insult by the Americans, by watching this video on following link.

http://frontierenews.it/2012/10/iraq-bruciati-tre-ragazzi-gay-in-nome-di-Allah-video/

This e-mail was sent by an Australian soldier that had combatted in Vietnam, to the bleeding hearts of those that cry out why those American marines urinated on the dead bodies.

I ask them to watch this video and then come back and speak with us.

To the officials, that cry out even louder. I ask them if they ever been in a combat zone or if they have seen one nearby.

Who are those that judge the soldiers, immediately after a battle or during one where you saw many of your fellow soldiers die.

Do not judge while sitting on a comfortable armchair, while the soldiers react during the fervor of a battle which can end their lives with the blink of an eye.

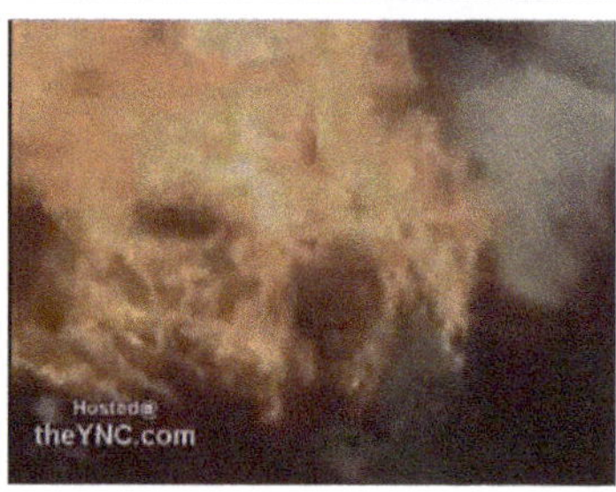

In this photo sequence, you can see a valiant fighter that is reading the reasons for a punishment. To his side there are another two heroes, one of which has in his hands a container filled with flammable liquid.

Once the sentence is read, the punishment is applied immediately with much efficiency.

The three unfortunate men are sprinkled with the liquid and pushed into a small bonfire.

Needless to say, they immediately catch fire.
Justice was made and...Allah Akbar.

THREE ALLAH AKBAR'S AND YOU'RE DEAD
This video was taken by our enemies.
The cameraman was filming one of his buddies which from one Allah Akbar to another, was launching mortars towards the English troops.
Unfortunately for him, he was not aware of our own new mortars. After three or four received hits, with its advanced technology, is capable of hitting back at the exact spot where the hostile ones came from.
Count the hits that Allah Akbar sends and you will see that on the fourth it will explode with all its military apparatus, hit right in the center by this portentous American mortar.
It would be very difficult to still be able to hear Allah Akbar from that man.
https://www.youtube.com/watch?v=_La199mD_hI

TRADITIONAL MEDICINE

The Pakistani Bilal, came in this country about two-months ago'. He begins to feel very bad, he goes to see a couple of doctors that are part of the national health service, but he continues to feel bad, so he decides to go to an Arab doctor. The doctor hands him a small container and tells him to go to the other room and do 'your thing' inside the container, then take this towel and cover your head and breathe deeply for five minutes. After that, Bilal tells the doctor that he feels much better, at least better than before.

"Doctor what did I have?", asks Bilal.

"Nothing bad, you were just suffering from homesickness", was the doctor's answer.

AUSTRIAN P.M ON THE TURKISH PEOPLE

I received this e-mail on the 22 of February, 2011. The person that sent it, also sent it to many other people. He recommended to watch this video before it gets deleted from you tube. It eventually got taken out. Not even I had the chance and pleasure of seeing it. Our friend writes:

It seems like the avalanche is falling off the mountain, destroying everything that is in its path. The Dutch prime minister began a speech by saying, the Islamic ideology is a very sick one. Shortly after that, the Norwegian prime minister sent back to Saudi Arabia over 200-million dollars, saying that if the Saudis want to build a mosque in Norway, they should first start by building churches in their country. Now the Austrian prime minister, accuses the Turkish regime to be made of criminals, and asks the Turkish ambassador to take his sick ideology and to go back to his country.

When, a few years ago', Salman Rushdy, said these things nobody believed him. The Arab extremists then put a price on his head. Now finally many are beginning to have second thoughts and think that Rushdy was correct In his thinking. But before Rushdy, another great journalist and writer, an Italian, had denounced the infiltration, a slow one, but steady one into Europe, by the Muslims.

Fallaci had coined in Eurabia terms, which nowadays should not sound absurd. For some of her books, Inshallah, Anger and Pride, and the Force of Reason, where the main theme is to fight the Islamic terrorists and their invasion of our dear Europe, she had received death threats by the usual suspects, which they still have not lost their bad habit of killing, or at least trying to kill whomever tries to write truths about them.

This is the link to the video:

http://www.youtube.com/watch?v=XRmgI_WXff0&feature=youtube_gdata_player

There will appear a beautiful black screen with red text...the video removed from you tube.

WELCOME TO BELGISTAN
http://www.cbn.com/tv/1509282970001

This interview could have easily taken place in Saudi Arabia, Iran, Pakistan, or even Afghanistan. In a place where the majority of Taliban people can be found and where their ideology is the law. Nobody would be amazed at what was said, in those places, instead this interview was given in Belgium where it's not exactly wrong to called it Belgistan. For those of you that do not know, in Brussels, there is a district being administrated by Muslims. This gentleman with a small hat and a long beard is speaking with the interviewer about Koranic law of the Sharia, as if it were a new law to be introduced to

Belgistan, which would be discussed at the parliament like any other law.

He speaks of it without fear or qualms whatsoever. He wishes that the Sharia will become law soon and to at least be enforced upon the Muslim population. If that were to take place we get to the absurd because in modern, emancipated countries such as Turkey, Morocco and Egypt, the Sharia is not applied, and a country right in the middle of Europe with old traditions like Belgium, would apply it, of course not for its Jewish, Christian and or Buddhists citizens but for the Muslims.

We shall see how this will end in Belgistan which it will inevitably become a sort of laboratory for the rest of the European countries to take notes as to what and what not should be done. So, according to statistics based on factual information, they say that at this pace, Brussels by 2030, will be of a Muslim majority.There are still 15-years to go, which is not that many.

lasociété
Bruxelles, musulmane en 2030 ?

MULTICULTURALISM

MULTIPLE WEDDING
Let's hope that none of the grooms make a mistake and take someone else's wife home.

ATTACK ON GRAVES OF ENGLISH SOLDIERS BY MUSLIM FUNDAMENTALISTS

http://www.liveleak.com/view?i=f03_1330829653

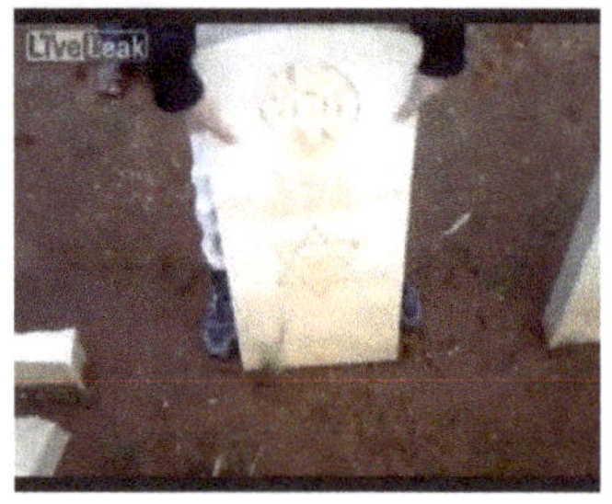

The Muslim suicide bombers will initiate a three-day strike beginning next Monday, because of a dispute in regards to as to how many virgins each one of them should have once dead. Meetings with Al Qaeda have not brought any resolution to the problem thus far. The problem arose the moment al Qaeda announced that each suicide bomber would have 25% less virgins waiting for him once dead, from 72 to only 54 virgins. A spokesman said that because of an increase of suicide bombers within the last year,
the consequence is that there are less virgins available on the other side. The reply by the suicide bomber's union, British Organization of Occupational Martyrs (B.O.O.M), answered by saying that al Qaeda's decision is unacceptable by its members, and for that reason they are on strike. The secretary general, Abdullah Amir, said the following to the press: "Our members literally work until death, for the Jihad's cause, we don't ask much in return, but to be treated in this manner, it is as if you're getting punched on the mouth."
Speaking from his hiding place in West Midlands, the executive commander of al Qaeda said the following: "I sympathize with our workers, but al Qaeda is not in the position to help them with this problem. Thanks to the depravity of the western world, there is a chronic lack of virgins in the afterlife. For this, I ask our workers to go back to work in order to help our common cause."

DO NOT DIE A VIRGIN

Good suggestion, do not die a virgin.
Up there are terrorists that are waiting for you.
I do not know in which country this manifesto appeared in and
the shirt with the same text, but it gets the idea across just fine.

THE DIFFERENCE

The young westerner takes his girlfriend for a ride, which shows a considerable lower back.
The other young man takes a poor sheep for a ride, which does not look too happy to do so.
TWO WORLDS APART AND IN SHARP CONTRAST

OSAMA BIN LADEN IN PARADISE, MEETS THE FIRST OF THE 72 VIRGINS RESERVED FOR HIM

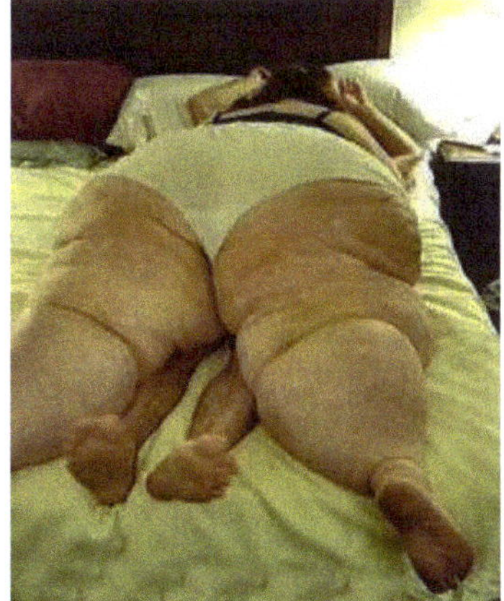

If they are all like that maybe it's best to do without.

HOW TO BEAT UP YOUR WIFE

The one that sent this e-mail, refers to the situation in some European countries in regards to Muslims. ''Where have all the organizations for women's rights gone to?''

It is unbelievable to see so many people that still believe that is a religion based on peace. I think just now Europe is beginning to realize that they have committed a huge mistake, for many years now, and now it is forced to fight off a total Islamization of the continent. The Muslims knew too well that they could never win Europe militarily, so now they are succeeding with a peaceful occupation, in nations where they are given documentation so that they can settle there.

I will add that we are still in time to do something about our continent and that we cannot hand it over to the Muslims. There is a video on you tube, where you see the interviewer asking an old man, a Muslim, how to treat a wife. The old man answers that a wife should be beaten in order to train her and make her docile. That way she will be obedient to her husband and owner. For that kind, the woman is like a horse or any other animal that becomes domesticated. Answering unconditionally to her owner, husband. He says one must not use blunt instruments when beating the woman, otherwise it will leave marks, scars, but to use your hands. Even with this method you must be careful, do not make a fist when hitting, leave your hands open, that way you won't leave any bruises. Another thing to remember, do not hit vital parts, because you might kill her, or maim her.

What could a man do then, if a woman is maimed or sick. The interview goes on for a while, with a lot of details, especially the ones explaining how to train her.

I would like to tell this gentleman, that women, even in Arab countries and third world countries, are making great strides. Is he too blind to see that women are often superior to men, for their intellectual capacity, abnegation and willpower.

They are superior to men in many professions.

The people that think like that old man that was interviewed, unfortunately, are a great majority of the Arab world and Islamic and it will be very difficult for them change the way they think, their convictions.

The only and last hope, are the young people. Everything is up to them. They must make a radical change that would finally bring both sexes to equal rights.

For the time being, they can do as they wish, but only in their country. Not in Europe and or Christian countries.

A TERRORIST CELL WAS DISCOVERED IN PUGLIA , SOUTH ITALY

An operational base in Puglia. With branches all over the world, even in Belgistan.

Those gentlemen were praying for a holy war, the jihad, and making proselytes in western countries in order to send them to the various theaters of war, such as Afghanistan, Chechnya, Iraq and lately even Syria. They were enticing racial hatred, and had a strong aversion for those western countries such as the U.S, Israel and even Italy, which the defined infidel countries.

The United States and Italy were called countries mongrels.

Those gentlemen from Morocco and Tunisia, living in Italy for many years, were enticing anti-Semitism, and racial hatred. They were hoping to fulfill planned attacks in western countries. The Carabinieri of ROS, made four arrests, three in Italy and one in Belgistan. Another two culprits are known to be back in Tunisia, buy I doubt they are idiots enough to come back here. Among the arrested there is the ex-imam from the mosque in Andria, the Tunisian, Hosni hachemi Ben Hassem, which was arrested in Belgistan. That gentleman was in contact with known Islamic terrorists, Essid Sami Ben Khemais, Ben Yahia Mouldi Ben Rachid and Ben Ali Mohammed. All with convictions. These beasts, besides showing satisfaction and joy for the earthquake that struck in Abruzzo, on the 7th of April, 2009, were criticizing the Muslim community in Italy that wanted to contribute with helping the victims of that disaster.

So, they were living a comfortable life in our home and hated us with no ifs and or buts.

Good people.

With all that we still have those that talk about welcoming them and integrating them. With those beasts, without offending the beasts, there is absolutely nothing we can do.

Everything we do is useless.

In regards to integration, I know many foreigners, which have integrated themselves with perfection within Italian society. They did everything by themselves, beginning with learning the language, frequenting Italian citizens, and learned a profession which would even be useful even if they decided to go back to their country someday. The others, the extremists, we need to send them to jail, to pay for their sins, without all the niceties that could be found in an Italian prison.

We should ask for advice from the jailers in North Korea, Cuba or even China. I think I would be very happy if such a cell would have been found in the People's Republic of China. You know how funny that would be, after a brief interrogation, followed by another brief investigation, having gathered the irrefutable evidence such as the Carabinieri ROS did, the Chinese would have closed the case in a very usual manner as it happens in that country, on your knees and a blow to the head and Allah u Akbar.

THE KILLING OF AN ENGLISH SOLDIER IN LONDON

This is another ugly act accomplished by Islamic fundamentalists in Europe, which has now become no man's land, or the land of the Islamic fundamentalists. If you write or say something that those people do not like, you are risking your life because those idiots have it in their heads to take control of our home. The people governing us still do not realize the absurd situation that we are in. We have to pay much attention to what we write and say, because besides the Islamists we have to deal with the do-gooders.

I would like to tell you a story, which happened to me last year while I was working in a hotel. In the lobby there was an Italian-Belgian gentleman, now living in Ostend.

He was travelling in Italy where he still has many relatives and friends. The hotel was full, I had placed a sign at the entrance explaining it, written in Italian, English and French.

An African couple, probably from Senegal, walked in and approached me at the front-desk and asked me for a double room. I answered that we were full so there were no rooms available.   Immediately the woman replied, in a tone of defiance, "You don't have rooms because I'm black?"

My instinctive response was, "Not because you are black, but because you are a stupid black woman." You did not read the sign that I attached at the entrance?"

They left looking for a room elsewhere. The Italian-Belgian client, surprised by what had happened but had liked the answer that I gave them, said to me that in Belgium he could not possibly give an answer such as the one I gave, because he would have big problems. I finally told that luckily I live in Italy and not Belgistan.

Going back to the poor English soldier that was killed by machete blows by a couple of Islamic fundamentalists. I think that those two had planned the attack, purposely hit his car with theirs, and once brought out of the car and on the ground, they hit him with a cleaver. Decapitating him while screaming out Allah u Akbar's.

The young man was wearing a t-shirt from the volunteer association "help for heroes", helping injured English soldiers in the battle field. He had just graduated from the Royal Artillery Academy, department of artilleryof her majesty, stationed in Woolvich. English police treated the matter as "an Islamic terrorist attack."

CONCLUSION

By reading this volume people will think that I am an exalted racist, but I can assure you with all tranquility that in my heart and soul, have never entertained feeling of hatred towards anyone because of religion or race.

This does not mean that I am willing to accept all that is said and done by those extremists of any color and tendency. If I say and write that I am not in agreement with many things and reveal concrete facts, which probably also touch on other people form other religions and races, it does not mean that I am a racist.

I Europe we have created a dangerous situation for the natives, in various places within the Old Continent, like in Belgium, Holland, England and France. Whomever denounces anything in regards to the immigrants is risking to be labeled a racist.

I will admit that those that create the most problems around the world are the Islamic fundamentalists, the jihadist, the proponents of a holy war, all those that want to impose Islam all over the planet, firmly believing that Islam is the only religion which leads directly to God.

For them, all other religions are not worthy to be compared to Islam, and all those that profess those other religions and are followers, are labelled as "infidels."

This habit of calling "infidels" all those that are not Muslims, goes back as far as the XIII century. At that time, the Ottomans had the habit to tie this epithet to all others that followed their own religions.

I think time has come to tell those people to leave us alone, in our world, with our habits. We would like to live our lives as we would like and not like they would like.

Those people should be careful not pulling the rope anymore, because in the end it could break with all its consequences.

We, westerners are capable of doing sublime things, but also very horrible things, things that we should be ashamed of. God should not want that someday, someone should decide to put an end to this situation and remedied all distortions and threats that are continuously hitting the western world. The continuous daily threats by people that want to hurt us.

I received an e-mail from Egypt, it was addressed to the president of the United States of America, Barack Obama, and it came from the person responsible for the Democratic Coalition of Egypt. Ahmed Said.

The writer of this e-mail is clearly an Arab from Egypt, non-Muslim. He had desired to explain to the president the complex situation that has arisen in that historic country in the recent past.

THE DEMOCRATIC EGYPTIAN COALITION ANSWERS TO THE PRESIDENT OF THE UNITED STATES OF AMERICA, BARACK OBAMA, AFTER ONE OF HIS STATEMENTS IN REGARDS TO THE PROTESTS THAT TOOK PLACE IN EGYPT IN RECENT MONTHS.

The Front for the National Salvation, a coalition of democratic parties, sends their objection to what the U.S president had said in regards to the violence and disorder that took place recently in Egypt. Led by Ahmed Said from The Free Egyptian Party.

They sent the following letter to the American administration in order to let the facts be known to them and the rest of the world, in regards to those events.

"Like many Egyptians, we have listened with much interest to your statement, in regards to the last events that have taken place in Egypt. As a representative of non-Islamic political forces in Egypt, we believe in the same fundamental values as those that the United States were founded on.

We have 7000-years of civilization and history which give us a particular identity. Ever since the Muslim brotherhood are in power, we are fighting a battle in order to preserve and maintain our history.

Let us inform you who in reality are the Muslim brotherhood of Egypt.

They are an illegal organization, that operate outside of Egyptian laws. It is funded by foreign powers, it recycles money in flagrant contempt of international laws.

Their goal is to rule the world via an Islamic Caliphate, because they believe in their absolute supremacy."

Those that think they are God's emissaries on earth, will never stop until they have subdued the whole world. Egypt is only the launching pad in order to realize their fascist dreams. With their international wings, they are able to get to many unsuspecting politician men.

They have utilized deceit, very soft speeches, international funds, and where is needed even violence to impose their ideas.

The role of the ousted president Mohammed Morsi, clearly shows how in less than a year they were able to take advantage of their people, not kept the promises they made to them, and changing the meaning of their laws by applying sort of constitutional diktat , monopolizing the judiciary system and the legislative power of the State.

All of this would have been enough to put Morsiunder investigation in any other democratic nation. So in the end, the Egyptians decided to take to the streets, so the second revolution of this century began, peaceful and unarmed, which started in June, 2013.   Their goal was to revoke Morsi's mandate and to reject to major role that was given to the Muslim Brotherhood.

The Egyptians deposed their president, not because he was not understood but because he broke his constitutional mandate, becoming another dictator just like the other predecessor that the same Egypt had deposed in January, 2011.

This was the will of the People that the west is now trying to reverse, using the pretense of wanting to bring democracy there, without interfering in their internal affairs.

I would like add, besides one's perception, the western media continue their one sided reporting, the Islamic.

We should make some facts be known, and truths. Since June 3, 2013, the day which president Morsi was taken out of office by the request of millions and millions of Egyptians, the European and American media, described the sit-in of Morsi's supporters, that paralyzed most of Cairo, like a "peaceful demonstration."

Those reporters choose to ignore everything else that was happening in Egypt.

Churches that were being burned and destroyed, indiscriminate killings and destruction of private and public property.

Mr. President, peaceful demonstrators don't go killing more than 50 policemen within a few hours. Mr. President, peaceful demonstrators do not attack a police station with RPG, they kill whoever is in front of them, take off their clothes and throw the bodies in the street.

Peaceful demonstrators do not threaten the Christians of genocide, just like the Muslim Brotherhood have stated many times during their hateful speeches in the squares of Cairo, during those "peaceful" demonstrations.

Peaceful demonstrators do not raise the black flag, symbol of Al Qaeda, while they walk in procession with photos of Bin Laden and Al Zawahiri on their chests. While the western media were following those sit-in live, more than 45 attacks against Christians were taking place all over Egypt and 19 Churches were destroyed and enflamed.

Some of those churches had been built in the sixth century and had immense value.

The list goes on, but we are certain that your secret service will inform you in details on everything that went on. The enclosed video should give you an idea as to the situation.

Mr. President, it is important that you see the truth, especially after the great suffering that you great American nation endured because of the Islamists, the loss of thousands of innocent Americans.

The Muslim Brotherhood and their Jihadists allies, have never known nor will they ever know peace.

It would be helpful to remember that those same persons had done three weeks of sit-in which began the day after the elections and not even after two-weeks had said that they would burn all of Egypt unless their candidate were to be proclaimed winner of the elections.

Mr. President, we are on the side of liberty and human rights, we are on the side for justice for all. We suffer when we see mother's crying for their dead sons and sons crying for their dead parents.

Mr. President, have you seen the video of the Muslim Brotherhood's supporters, which throw a 14-year-old boy from a six-story building. What sort of peaceful demonstrators are they?

A mother died of pain when she saw the video-clip of her son being thrown off. She didn't even have time to mourn for her son.

Today Mr. President you have chosen to consider only part of the picture and to punish the Egyptians by cancelling the program Bright Star.

Fine Mr. President, Bright Star does not mean anything for the majority of Egyptians, however, we are more concerned with the misunderstanding and deceit of the American people.

The Egyptians have always been with the American Nation, when the United States were attacked by the Islamist terrorists, because we are for those who love liberty for all, just like the American people.

The only difference is that we have always been deprived of those principles and rights.

Is it asking too much for the Egyptians to seek support by the Americans during their war on terror?

How can the same group of people be called terrorists in the U.S.A, and peaceful demonstrators in Egypt?

How can it be that the Americans will never negotiate with those terrorists, but the same Americans are asking the Egyptians to negotiate with them, even to make an alliance with them in order to build a more modern Egypt?

Mr. President, the interests for peace within the region, would better be served by the real lovers of peace and real democratic people.

At last Mr. President, we hope that this letter will attract your attention, because right now we represent the majority, our current government represent us, civil and liberal forces.

Let's hope that you will find interesting our message in order to investigate and inform yourself even more. When you will do it, we will be ready to come to you with a small delegation, in order to explain to you all sides of this very complicated situation in Egypt.

We are certain that you have comprehended that the Egyptians are a great people and deserve a great future.

THE FOLLOWING LETTER I RECEIVED FROM THE CENTER OF CHRISTIAN CULTURE

THE ISLAMIC EXPANSION IN EUROPE

In front of the possibility that the Parliament of the European Union accepts within the Union other countries such as Turkey, which besides being Asian land, it is light-years away from the culture and institutions of Europe. We ask the responsible ones, to reflect on the dangerous consequences that this decision could bring about.

Not only for obvious reasons, economic, the entry of at least 70-million people being below the average level of poverty, but mainly because Turkish culture is decisively and Islamic one, with all the consequences that it would bring about.

Certainly it will not be the Turkish Muslims to adapt to the laws and institutions of Europe, if anything, it will be the Islamic culture to impose itself in the West, even with violence just like centuries past. Like the Bin Laden types that do not hesitate in professing this.

Make no mistake in thinking that we can resolve these issues with the much talked about "dialogue" method, because for us westerners having lived within the Christian faith, dialogue means to be able to cohabitate with people with other religious beliefs, that is obvious, but for the Muslim world that is impossible, simply because the essence of Islamic culture was founded on the most inflexible intransigence between faith and politics. Between divine right and the rule of law, this way making it impossible to find and agreement based on man's human rights.

The European Court of Justice, on the 31 of July, 2001, affirmed with a sentence the incompatibility of the Koranic law, Sharia, with the Convention for human rights.

A couple of expert of Koranic law, Bausani and Fahad, authors of books such as Islamism, they inform us that Islam, without admitting to God's rational knowledge and of the world, bases its knowledge, only on faith, as absolute value, meaning, on blind faith all in the name of the Koran, where one conception prevails of the fatalistic and sensual life.

However, the biggest difficulty for an understanding with Islam, is not only about the religious aspect, but as we have mentioned before, it goes against the laic environment, the civil one, social and legal, men's vision, life and society, the family, all completely disrupted.

Our Center of Christian Culture, it proposed to expose this argument in a briefly manner, along two directions:

1. Contents of Islamic faith
2. 1400 years of Islamic history.

THE CONTENTS

THE KORAN AND MOHAMMED

The only source of Islamic doctrine, Sharia, is the Koran, Book divinity delivered to Mohammed's followers.

Mohammed, (570-632), was an Arab camel handler, but mostly he was a restless warrior, which together with his faith for Allah, the principal element of his religious beliefs. He had ten wives, without counting his concubines, and sanctioned the right of men to freer polygamy at the expense of women. (Kor. IV.3).

Mohammed felt that he was invested with the duty to force men into idolatry, subduing them to believe in one God only, Allah. (Islam means submission).

A distant God, impenetrable to human intellect, absolute arbiter of everything, which demands punishment for human error, especially women, even with mutilation and violent death. A God, which men has no liberty nor responsibility.

Islam does not allow a rational knowledge of God and of nature, so it bases its knowledge only on faith, as an absolute value. This is opposite of catholic theology, which teaches that God is known to human not only by Creation, but mostly through the Revelation of Jesus Christ.

The God that is invoked by the Muslims, has nothing to do with the Christian's God, which to begin with is, Father full of goodness and mercy, image and likeness, a God that loves men so much as to entrust him with one precise Commandment, Love.

Islam refuses the principal dogmas of Christianity, those of Unity and Trinity of God, incarnation, death and resurrection of Jesus Christ, the divine maternity of Maria, the divine revelation of the gospel, the divine institution of the church, of the priesthood, the sacraments, etc.

SOME EXAMPLES ON THE CIVIL SIDE

Islam, does not know the concept of "person" as a legal entity, a concept typically Christian, but only the right of "Ummah", of the community. Islam does not conceive the idea of the family as a free choice between a man and a woman, but only as a unilateral choice, of the man, which decides to buy one or more women, which are then excluded from decision making all together. They can be repudiated and have their kids taken away at any moment.

Islam does not conceive the concept of liberty, nor persona or that of association.

He who does not revere Mohammed or objects to any passage of the Koran, will be killed without a trial. Carlo Sgorgon, in more than one article on the daily newspaper "Il Tempo", says that the typical Mohammed follower, does not integrate himself, demands that each one of his religious customs be respected, but he does not concede anything to the Christian, because the real Muslim does not understand tolerance, and never grants anything. You do what he wants or we arrive at war. Islam, denies any other human law, every social progress because the Koran is the only religious and civil law, unchangeable and untouchable.

This forces the Islamic society to refuse the notion of any natural and legislative right, which there are no other rights but only the ones provided by the Koran.

The Muslim leaders, the Caliphs, emirs, etc.. are some of the richest men in the world, because they are owners or control most oil production in the world, but most of their citizens live under miserable conditions and backwardness, mainly because those rich men do not want to or do not know how to utilize their riches in the name of progress, which for the Christians it is an important, dutiful aspect men's life on earth.

Islam, divides the world in "Islamic territory", and "war territory for the infidels", which has to be conquered with the holy war, an obligation imposed by God to all Muslims, until the whole world becomes submissive to Allah.

Submissive to the Islamic State. Even the silent penetration of Muslims by immigration is another method for them to conquer the world. (Vignelli."The Silent Invasion", Minotauro edition.

Mons Fouad Twal, archbishop of Tunis, in an interview for the magazine Nuntium, said that Islam is the bearer of a model for a society aimed at a theocratic and totalitarian state, founded on the Sharia and the jihad. The holy war is not a marginal aspect of Islam, but it constitutes a real obligation for the believer, follower, also against those that choose to interpret it reductively, as if it were only spiritual warfare. The archbishop says that the texts and facts are clear: "It is about a real war against the infidels, which means against anyone that is not Muslim. It is the religion of force, because it imposes itself only by force and yields only in front of violence. Islamism and violence are integral parts of Islam". In fact he recites verses of the Koran: "War is prescribed even if you do not like it". (Kor. 2, 221)

"Kill the idolaters wherever you find them". (Kor. 9,5)

"Prophet! Fight against all infidels and the hypocrites and be hard on them. (Kor. 66,9).

In this war the infidels cannot claim any inherent rights, because Islam does not recognize non-Muslim persons or States as legal entities, also it does not recognize prisoner's rights which are the winner's "property". Slavery, which was abolished in the Christian West, is entitled in Islamic States because it is officially recognized in the Koran. (Kor. 2,221).

How has Islam spread? By fighting wars. Its founder, Mohammed, gave the first example, slaughtering the people that were idolaters, which had to be brought to the faith of only one God.

After only 20-years from the death of the Prophet, the Arab Muslims, led by the Caliph Caleb, conquered Palestine, all of Christian-Africa along the Mediterranean, defeated the Persian empire. From Morocco they went on to Spain, defeating the Visigoths. From there they would have conquered the rest of Europe had they not been stopped in Poitiers by Carlo Martello, in 732. Those Muslim Arabs, that remained in Spain after the defeat of Poitiers, built a strong community, which by interacting with other civilizations such as the Greek-Byzantine and the Roman-Christian, were able to contribute the most in the fields of philosophy and science.

Still, the pugnacious nature of Islam was emerging more and more, constituting a real threat for the rest of Europe.

After seven centuries, in 1240, with San Ferdinand III of Castile, and in 1481, with king Ferdinand of Aragon, the Arabs were definitely expelled from the Iberian Peninsula and the rest of Europe. From the XV century, Islamic culture began a inexorable decline, while the threat of the Turks was advancing, also Muslims but very different from the Arabs, which the Ottomans were keeping at a distance.

The Ottomans were seriously threatening the Christian civilization, which with the defensive spirit of western culture were able to stop their advance by defeating the Ottomans at the battle of Lepanto, in 1571. In Vienna as well, in 1683, and in Belgrade in 1717.

Whenever they want to compare the Crusades fought by the Christians against Islam, between the XII and XIII century, to

the so-called Islamic holy wars, one clarification is necessary, the Crusades had nothing similar to the Islamic wars,
not necessarily because of the war strategy, obviously, but a basic fundamental concept. The crusades were military expeditions, granted not to impose the Catholic faith, but to free the holy places occupied by the Muslims which were blocking access. Death penalty to the infidel pilgrims. There would not have been Crusades had Islam respected the Christian lands. That among the Crusaders, abuse and brutality took place, is a fact, however, many historians such as Jean Richard and Rene' Grousset, were in agreement as to Crusades having left an historic mark of epic proportions for many reasons, obviously the first of which because the whole Christian world had united "as one heart", with the only intent to defend that heritage of faith, of culture and of sacred places, marked by the presence of the doctrine of Christ. There was the awareness that each Christian and the whole community had an immense treasure to defend, to pass on intact to posterity.
A treasure which, if the circumstances required, needed to be defended by all means.

ISLAM TO THE PRESENT DAY
The magazine Mashrek International, made public the resolutions taken by the Islamic Council that took place in Lahore, Pakistan, in 1980, which established that the entire Middle East had to be totally Islamic by the year 2000. The popular groups which do not belong to the Islamic creed have to be destroyed. In fact, it happened that way. The Islamist, OnoratoBucci, describes the situation in regards to this dramatic situation worldwide:

From Lebanon, in 15-years of civil war, without counting the slain dead, we had a dramatic exodus of over 2-million Christians, Maronites and other confessions, towards Europe and the Americas. Not less dramatic, Bucci continues, is the situation in other Middle Eastern countries, Egypt, Syria, Turkey and more recently Sierra Leon, Sudan, Nigeria, Moluccas islands, Isle of Fear, and all of Indonesia, that have undergone untold killings, which the majority of the population was prior mainly of Christian faith, now by force, almost all Muslim.

Even in the Philippines, meek Catholic state, has seen a great number of Muslims enter and now want to create a Muslim state, by way of wars, persecutions and killings. See Mindanao and the archipelago of Sulu. Misery and hunger in Africa, are caused in gran part by the Islamic advance in those places where as the missionaries are denouncing, were forced to escape, where the terrorists destroy all that was built by those people, such as wells, water systems, schools, hospitals, etc.

The tragedy of the "twin towers", in America, the massacre in Nigeria of 250 Christians caused by an innocent phrase on Mohammed, the horrible slaughter of kids at a school in Chechnya, the continuous attacks and massacres all over the world, even among their compatriots, only because as they say, by being too westernized. These are all events that unfortunately happen on daily basis.

Events which Muslims are proud of because it is part of their Koran's "creed".

It wants the holy war, a sacred duty for every Muslim, until the whole world is submissive to Allah. There are many reasons to believe that even in Italy and the rest of Europe, similar things can happen. The blood toll by Christians killed all over the world, mainly where the Sharia is imposed, is about 160.000

victims per year, documented by Antonio Socci in his book "The persecuted Christians".

Mons. Bernardini, Archbishop of Izmir, in Turkey for over 40-years, declared: "During a meeting on Islamic-Catholic dialogue, an authoritative Muslim personality, said to the participants "Thanks to your democratic laws we will invade you, thanks to our religious laws we will dominate you". The prelate adds that it is believable because the dominance has already begun with the petrodollars, used not to create work in those poor African and Middle Eastern countries, but to build mosques all over the Christian lands, by way of continuous immigration.

How can we not see in this, the Archbishop continues, a clear program of expansion and of recapture?

In fact, Muslims don't know how to create industries, but are magnificent warriors that do not fear death, and we ask ourselves, baffled, how is it possible that these fears never arise in the minds of our politicians?".

TO DEFEND OURSELVES OR SURRENDER

In front of this prospective what significance do words such as "dialogue" or "peace" have? Maybe it means a passive attitude or defeatist as the greatest good to be achieved, thanks to which we could save our lives, while losing our own identity and freedom? Such a conception of peace does not only mean a refusal of war but it becomes a doctrine, a lifestyle, an irenic myth and relativist for which there exists to truth to defend. This false peace, in name only, where not only the weapons are buried, principles, values, faith, the honor and culture of a whole people, it all does nothing but to model a whole puppet race at the mercy of the bullies.

As Winston Churchill foresaw, at the conference in Monaco, in 1938, when the English Prime Minister, Chamberlain, gave in to Hitler's blackmails in order to avoid war.

He put it this way: "You called for peace with dishonor, so you will have war with dishonor".

History proved him right.

Two luminaries of Christianity, the Fathers of the church of San Augustine and San Thomas Aquinas, made clear the concept of a just war, "It must be understood as an evil, which at times is necessary in order to restore justice, peace and avoid more evils".

Very interesting as well, the booklet "Just war, holy war", by Roberto de Mattei Ed Piemme.

WHICH FUTURE FOR EUROPE?

What can our Europe expect which has disowned its roots, its faith, its culture, its civilization. The wonderful beauty of its monuments, churches. Its exemplary right based on the dignity of the person, the family?

History shows that civilizations so degenerated, have all ended up in the hands of their enemies.

This European Union that refuses and tramples its Christian roots, which have made glorious throughout the centuries, does not hesitate to give up its catholic churches to the Muslims all in the name of ecumenism, to take away its crucifix in the name of tolerance, and make a show of atheism and sexual licentiousness outreach.

This European Union which pretends to legislate on everything, from the reproduction system of strawberries to the human beings, considered goods to be eliminated whenever it begins to "deteriorate".

This European Union that is destroying the family in its perennial values, which allocates money for easy abortions, for the control of births all over the world.

This Europe which demands to legitimize any transgressive libertinism, presenting itself as the "sex arbitrate", and even arriving at depriving children a normal family life in order to accommodate certain couple's life styles.

This Europe which wants to welcome Turkey in, at all costs, with all of 70-million Islamists at our door with full rights. If the Turks never wanted to recognize the genocide of 1915 against the Armenian people, under what values or accords, or culture, could they ever establish an alliance with Europe?

This European Union without a soul, that stained itself with apostasy and started inexorably towards her own destruction. Islam, which in past centuries did not succeed in conquering Europe, thanks to the power Christianity, Cross and Rosary, is now succeeding with the same iniquitous laws of the Europeans, also because militarily speaking there would be no challenge whatsoever, considering the huge technological gap that separates our old and dear Europe from the Muslim world. Concluding: Like in the Old Testament, God allowed the chosen people to be imprisoned and deported to Babylonia, because of their repeated infidelities. So now we find ourselves in front of an alternative that whether we like it or not, will mark our future. Either we are faithful to Christ, in particular the Crucifix, without fear to bear witness, by exposing it in our homes, at the hospitals, workplaces, or the inevitable consequence will not be that of living in peace in a "laic" state, meaning free of all religions and traditions, like some of the politicians would like for us to believe, but finally and inevitably slaves of a theocratic State, which would be the worst tyranny of all forms of Totalitarianism which have conquered Europe, especially Eastern Europe, this past century.

The example of our ancestors which arrested the Islamic advance with weapons and soldiers inferior to their enemies, but with the strength of their faith, should be an incentive to imitate them.

The Carolingian Prince, Carlo Martello, which defeated the Muslims at Poitiers, in 732, attributed to the Madonna his memorable victory, taken place on a Saturday in October, and as a sign of gratitude fund the Orders of Chivalry, consecrated to the Virgin Mary.

The rulers of Spain, in 1240 and in 1481, succeeded in the difficult feat of removing the Moors from Europe.

They did that by believing in the Virgin Mary along the rest of the population.

In Lepanto, 1571, the very powerful Turkish fleet was defeated by the few Christian vessels, ill-equipped, but thanks to the Holy Rosary which Pope Saint Pius V had asked all Christians to pray with.

In Vienna, 1683, Pope Innocent XI, commanded all Christians to pray to the Virgin Mary in order to find the right commander in order to guide the soldiers to fight against the Turks, perched on the hills of Vienna, ready to launch a final decisive attack. John III Sobieski, King of Poland, felt inspired to go to Vienna, decided to lead the battle. Before descending on the field, participated as an altar boy at the Mass celebrated by Father Marco d'Aviano, beatified by Pope John Paul II. Imploring Christ's help for the intercession of the Virgin Mary. It is narrated that Father Marco, while raising the Crucifix towards the hills of Vienna, the Christian soldiers, as they were descending on the field of battle, felt unexpected strength which routed the Turks. All unexplainable, seeing the exiguous number of our troops and the scary, armed to their teeth, Turkish troops.

In Belgrade, 15th August, 1717, Eugenio of Savoy, arrested the Turkish advance after being consecrated to the Virgin Mary, offering Her all the suffering of his troops, Jesus Christ had said "Courage, I have conquered the whole world".

So, only in the name of God would be possible to beat an enemy of this magnitude, in fact, the Virgin Mary and Fatima, he assured: "In the end, my Immaculate Heart will triumph".

We should believe in His words, even if at this moment it is difficult to see it realized.

I received this e-mail on the 9th of August, 2013, and it's entitled "More….Muslims".

It is written by an Australian citizen manifesting his frustration for an absurd situation that has come to be not only in his country but in all of the Western world.

Probably the only ones that are saved from this problem are the countries that used to be or that still are communist.

Those countries have a vision of Democracy and individual liberties that are far removed from our way of thinking.

It would be enough just to read the speech given at the Duma by president Vladimir Putin and was given a standing ovation for over 4 minutes.

I have already mentioned this beautiful speech given by the president of the Russian Federation at the beginning of this book, and I ask myself if a Minister of the so-called Western Europe could ever give such a decisive speech which runs parallel with the actual laws implemented in Muslim countries.

NEW LAWS ON IMMIGRATION

1.

There will not be bilingual programs in our schools.

2.

All exams will be given in the language of this country.

3.

All governmental affairs will be done in our language.

4.

The non-residents shall not have voting rights. It does not matter how long they have been in this country.

5.

The non-citizens shall never have political appointments.

6.

The foreigners shall never be a weight on our society, No economic assistance. No food stamps. No free health care. No to the various government programs assisting foreigners.

7.

The foreigners can invest in this country, but the amount should be a minimum of 40.000 times the daily minimum wage.

8.

If a foreigner comes to this country and desires to buy land, their option would be very limited. Land in front of lakes and rivers will be reserved for citizens born in this country.

9.

Foreigner shall not engage in manifestations of protest. They shall not wave any foreign flags and shall not engage in political organizations.

10.

If a foreigner enters this country illegally, he will be searched for and when apprehended will be imprisoned until his expulsion will take place.

Laws to severe and harsh?

The listed laws above are actual laws in force at this time in Muslim countries.

I must admit in all honesty that I like them, very much.

The do-gooders, should ask themselves why such laws that are in force in the countries where most of the immigrants come from should not be applied in Western countries, which are forced to legally welcome them and most of the time illegally.

When can we hope that such laws will be enforced, beginning with Belgium, Holland, France, Great Britain, which seem to me that at the moment are the ones doing worse.

I am not against immigration, foreigners are welcome in our world, as long as they come legally.

For the foreigners that come to the Western countries, are some suggestions and regulations to respect, may they be the same regulations that are asked to a Westerner travelling or deciding to move to Pakistan, Saudi Arabia, Iraq or any other Arab and or Muslim country.

Here following is what it is about.

Find a sponsor.

Find a place where to sleep.

Find a job.

Live here while respecting our laws and customs.

Pay your taxes.

Learn the language of the country that is welcoming you.

Please do not ask us to donate to you and your numerous families our benefits, our indemnity and our lifetime savings.

I would like to repeat myself.

These "suggestions and advice", just listed, are actual laws and regulations in force in Arab and Muslim countries in general, with the only probable exceptions being Turkey, Morocco and the Gulf Emirates.

If a Westerner would venture to not observe those laws and regulations he or she would find themselves in big trouble, which would be extremely difficult to get out of.

Now I would like to talk about an e-mail that refers to the French soccer national team.
I will first state that I am a sportsman, and that whenever I follow a sport I admire all that the athletes are able to do. I follow their prowess, their will, their sacrifice and I certainly do not stop to look at the color of their skin.
I have admired the exploits of Jessy Owens, Joe Frazier, Carl Lewis, Fausto Coppi, Nino Benvenuti, Ascari, Villeneuve, Carlos Monzon, Joe Louis, Rocco Marcheggiano (Marciano), Nadia Comaneci, Zhu Jianhua, Abebe Bikila, Sebastian Coe, Kipkonge Keino, Haile Gebrselassie, Paul Tergat, Mohammed Farah, Usain Bolt, Carlos Duran, Pele, Schiaffino, Manny Pacquiao, Eusebio. Garrincha, Hector "Macho" Camacio, Puskas, Baggio, Di Stefano, Sugar Ray Leonard, Giacomo Agostini, Carlo Ubbiali, Ray Sugar Robinson, Niki Lauda, Michael Schumacher, Emile Griffith, in short, for me athletes of this level deserve infinite respect and much admiration. They are special people that deserve everyone's respect for the sacrifice and commitment behind every success. What to say then of the singers of color, that have delighted and continue to delight us with their stupendous voices, with their ability to interpret the beautiful and famous songs that we all know?
How can we not admire Louis Armstrong, Fats Domino, Ella Fitzgerald, Steve Wonder, Little Richard, The Platters, Diana Ross, Nat King Cole, Ray Charles, Harry Belafonte and the three singers that I call queens, Gloria Gaynor, Tina Turner and Whiney Houston?

The race, the color of the skin, the religion and their political associations don't mean a thing which a small obtuse and ignorant minority would like.
I admire unconditionally all those people and I don't care to know what color their skin is and what religion they profess.
That does not mean that certain things should be said, without fear of upsetting anyone that might think of it as racism.

I received this e-mail which shows the French national soccer team from two different periods. In 1959 and fifty-years later, in 2010.
The only white player is Ribery, but in the team photo of 2010 he was not included.

FRENCH SOCCER TEAM 2010

French Soccer Team 2010

I have nothing against those players, in fact, I admire them for their bravery and sportsmanship, but it does not seem normal to me that a major national team such as the French team, would have only one native player on its roster.

With us, in Italy, in 1996, Prodi, in power a little over four months, the do-gooders had the great idea to elect a Miss Italy, not your typical Italian and or Mediterranean-looking young woman, but a non-native Italian and of typical beauty of the Caribbean Islands.

It's as if in Ghana they would elect a Miss Ghana, a beautiful girl from Sweden, which by no means would be able to represent this Central African Republic.

I would like to add a final observation, I have nothing against Miss Mendez, which I find beautiful and sweet, but I want to reiterate my concept, that this beautiful woman cannot represent Italian women, which have very different characteristics from the beautiful Caribbean young woman which was elected Miss Italy in 1996, with Prodi in power.

It comes to mind, the killing of animals by Muslims and Israelites in order to achieve the Halal and Kosher products.

The term Halal is Arabic, which means lawful, permitted, in contrast with the word Haram, which means prohibited.

For the Jews, the equivalent term is Kosher.

The animal is hung on hooks while alive and conscious, and it is slain.

The poor beast will bleed to death and its agony will last over ten-minutes.

This way, the body of the beast, losing all its blood, will lose all the impurities that it contains.

This barbaric and inhumane method, was prohibited in the small but great Switzerland, while In Italy the animal prior to being slain should be numb with a hit on the head with a special pistol. I say should be, because personally I don't think the slaughterhouse workers respect this regulation.

In anyway, for Italy it's a step forward.

The Islamic and Jewish slaughter methods as it happens in Muslim countries and in Israel, produces unnecessary suffering for the animals which are forced to stay conscious during their bleeding to death, without being numbed first.

The killing takes place by cutting the trachea, esophagus, carotid artery, jugular vein, vagus nerve, by a rapid motion of the ritual butcher, which uses a knife with a very sharp blade.
According to religious sources, Muslim and Jewish, the animal loses consciousness instantly so it does not feel the pain.
If they say so...
I try to imagine what happens in France, Great Britain, Belgium, Holland, on this argument, but I think in those four European countries the slaughtering of animals is done no more no less as it is done in Jeddah, Riyadh, Taif, Baghdad, Teheran, Islamabad and all the other cities within the immense Muslim world.
It seems to me very superfluous to talk about animal rights organizations either in Muslim countries or in Europe. Those organizations are a little like the feminists, you never hear them protest as to the treatment of Muslim women here in Italy, but they are always ready to take position if a case happens in a country like the U. S or any other country that is not in their favor. In Italy the chronicles are full of stories of Muslim women who are abused, harassed, mutilated, and in some cases even killed, by those who should be their protectors, their fathers, husbands and brothers.
At this point I have finished my work.
I continuously receive e-mails in regards to many subject, but often about Muslims.
I cannot keep on adding to the book, otherwise I will never be able to finish it.
I hope that someone will find it interesting and likeable enough to read it.
I simply collected and introduced all the e-mails to you which I have received within the last 4-years.

I am very aware that for some people this body of work will not be to their liking and would also find it hateful and factious, but I'm not writing this for them. I am reporting the opinion of many people throughout the world, which for the most part I don't even know.

However, everything that I'm reporting has been circulating online for many years, it is not secret nor hidden material.

All the e-mails that I have received were also sent to thousands of other people, which have read and in many cases sent them to their friends and people they knew all over the world.

I suggest to those that will be contrary to this work, not to read it and to leave in peace those that have the time and will to read it.

This behavior is part of individual liberties, and ultimately, Democracy, even if I am aware that for some this term is unknown.

I had decided to end my work right at this point, but I had received another 4 e-mails which I could not overlook.

I have been waiting for the book cover which is running late so I decided to add these other four e-mails.

Following I inserted three of them and the fourth I included where I talk about the burqa. It is the one that talks about a compliment being given to a woman in a burqa with her three kids, the problem is that the woman only had only one child and not three as the observer believed.

Let's start with the first which I received on the 26th of February, this year.

The title is "TO ADOPT A TERRORIST".

The Canadians surely know how to handle all the gripes and suggestions that reach the various government offices in Ottawa, from the Canadian citizens.

Following is the explanation in the e-mail:

A Canadian woman with very liberal views, has written many letters to the central government in Ottawa, worrying about the treatment Taliban prisoners were receiving in Afghanistan and in particular at the Afghanistan Correctional System Facilities. The lady received this reply:

NATIONAL DEFENCE HEADQUARTER

M GEN. GEORGE R. PARKES BLD 15 NT

101 COLONEL BY DRIVE

OTTAWA ON. KIA OK2

CANADA

Dear Citizen, thanks for your most recent letter, in which you clearly express your worries in regards to the treatment reserved to the Taliban prisoners.

Also your worries about the Al Qaeda terrorist's treatment, which were captured by the Canadian forces in combat zones and were then transferred to the Afghan army and are at present under the control of the Afghan officials at the Afghanistan Correctional System Facilities.

Your opinion was given serious consideration here in Ottawa, and you will be happy to hear that thanks to the worries and suggestions by citizens such as yourself, we have created a new department here at the Ministry of Defense.

This new department will be named LARK. Liberals Accept Responsibility for Killers Program.

Following the guidelines of this new program, we have decided to house some of these terrorists at the homes of our Canadian citizens, especially the ones that worry about their treatment at the hands of the officials in Afghanistan.

This will take place under the citizens own responsibility.

Your personal prisoner has been chosen and is ready to be transferred under heavy security to your home in Toronto, the following Monday.

Ali Mohamed Ahmed Bin Mahmud, your prisoner, should find the right treatment which you have worried about and expressed in your letters under your detention.

You will be happy to know that we will make weekly visits to your home to make sure that your treatment for the prisoner is adequate enough as your advice and worries in your letters.

Knowing that Ahmed is a very asocial person and extremely violent, we hope that your tact and sense of things for what you have termed "ATTITUDINAL PROBLEMS", will help you overcome those character issues.

Probably you are right in describing those problems as mere cultural differences.

We have understood that you have in mind to offer Ahmed advice and after-school at home but we really suggest to you to hire some assistants.

Professional assistants that is, used to confronting any type of emergency.

We also would like to advise you to alert every Jewish friend, the whole neighborhood and all of your relatives of your guest, otherwise he might get upset and become very violent, at the end, we are sure that you are going to be able to reason with him.

Ahmed is also an expert in the production of explosives, using common household products, so it is also advised that you keep your common household products under lock and key, unless in your opinion that might offend him.

Your adopted terrorist is very efficient in combat with his bare hands, and also very capable of ending a life as if it were a pen.

We advise you not to ask him to demonstrate his skills, not in your home nor anywhere you think you might take him in order to reorganize his life in our country.

Ahmed will not love to deal with you or your daughters unless it is for sex.

He thinks women have absolutely no rights, they are his property, they cannot refuse sexual requests. This is a topic particularly sensitive for him, which has demonstrated violent behavior towards women that have merely refuse what clothing he wanted them to wear, without saying, especially the burqa.

I am sure that in time you will be able to appreciate the anonymity and warmth that this piece of apparel typically Arab and Muslim can offer.

Keep in mind that all of this has to do with respecting his culture and religious creed, has described in your last letter.

Take good care of Ahmed and remember that we will always have an advisor ready to help you in case of difficulty, while Ahmed tries to get accustomed to the Canadian culture.

Thanks again for your interest.

We appreciate very much all the persons such as yourself, that keep informed as to the right way for us to do our duty, and all of our soldiers.

Good luck and God Bless.

Cordially Gordon O. Connor

National Defense Minister

I think that the reply that the Minister of Defense gave to that caring citizen worried about the treatment of the Taliban people and terrorists in general, to try and care a little more for the Canadian soldiers engaged with other coalition soldiers in defending us from those assassins.

This second e-mail which I received on the 5th of March, 2014, is entitled "What is an infidel".

What you are about to read is a true story, and its author Rick Mathes is a well- known operator at the prison's administration.

A man that walks with God will always reach his destination.

If you are determined than you have a purpose.

The Muslim religion is the fastest growing religion in the United States, particularly within the minorities.

Last month I participated in an annual training course which is required in order to maintain a high-level of security in the prisons.

During the session there was an intervention by three representatives, the Roman Catholic Church, Protestant and Muslim, and each one of them got to explain and talk about their creed. I was particularly interested as to what the Muslim representative had to say.

The Imam, gave a good presentation explaining the basics of Islam, including a video. After the presentation we were allowed to ask questions.

When my turn came up to ask a question, I asked the following, "Would you please correct me If I'm wrong, but many Imams have declared a holy war, Jihad against all the infidels of the world, and that the Muslims, by killing an infidel, which is a commandment for all Muslims, would be guaranteed a place in paradise. If this is truly the case, would you give me the definition of infidel?".

There was no embarrassment for my question, without hesitation the Imam answered, "non-believer".

"So, let me understand better and with certainty, all the followers of Allah were commanded to kill those that do not embrace your religion, in order to assure themselves a place in paradise, is this correct?".

The expression on his face changed from that of a man with authority to the one of a child caught with his hands on the jelly jar.

Then very timidly he answered, yes.

"Dear Sir, I have a real problem imagining the Pope ordering all the Catholics to kill because of religious views or any other view. Doctor Stanley ordering all the Protestants to kill, in order to assure themselves a place in paradise".

The Muslim literally remained with his mouth closed, without a word.

"Even I have a problem to be you friend the moment you and your colleagues tell your followers to kill me. Let me as another question. You prefer your Allah who tells you to kill me in order to assure yourself a place in paradise, or my Jesus who tells me to love you and go to Paradise, and would also like for you to be up there with me?"

You could hear a pin drop while the Imam was twisting his head backward.

Needless to say, the organizers and promoters of this course were not too pleased with my behavior towards the Imam, exposing the truth about the Islamic creed.

In less than 20-years there will be enough Muslim voters in Australia in order to be able to elect a Muslim Prime Minister.

I think that in Australia and the rest of the Western world, everyone should read my letter and draw the consequences.

I read it with much interest, even though I was aware of those facts since many years. I would like to add one thing.

Do not sleep and do something, in order that what Rick Mathes has predicted will happen in 20-years, happens.

Know that their birth rate compare to ours, is 9 to 1, and twenty-years goes by faster than you can imagine. To the skeptical ones, I ask to make a simple calculation, starting with the present Muslim and non-Muslim population in Australia. Calculate the 9 to 1 ratio, that should leave us thinking a little bit of the situation that the Western world is in.

One last news item that should let us reflect some more and worry about our future and our kids future.

In Brussels, Belgium, there is already a district that is administrated by Muslims. Brussels finds itself in the heart of Europe.

This happens because unlike what we do, the Muslims all vote for their Muslim candidate.

Voters from countries that are far away from one another, such as Morocco and Bangladesh, with different customs and traditions, speaking different languages, countries who in the past have been at war with one another, when the time to vote comes, they give their preference to the Muslim candidate, no matter where he's from, only because they share the same religion.

I received this last e-mail on the 9th of March, 2014. It is the reply by an American citizen to a speech given by Barack Obama, in Cairo, on the 4th of June, 2012.

The citizen is contesting what Obama had said in regards to the Muslims, who have always been close to America and are part of American Heritage.

The President said exactly as follows, "I am aware of the fact that Islam has always been part of American history".

Here follows the answer:

"Dear Mr. Obama, have you ever seen a Muslim hospital?

Have you ever known a Muslim orchestra?

Have you ever seen a Muslim marching band, together with other bands at parades?

Have you ever known a Charity, an organization for the needy, by Muslims?

Have you ever seen Muslims shake hands with a scout?

Have you ever seen a Muslim do something to contribute positively to the American lifestyle?

The answer is no.

Ask yourself why.

Where were those Muslims when the first "pilgrim-pioneers" arrived in America? Strange, I thought they were the native American-Indians.

Maybe it was the Muslims that celebrated the first Thanksgiving.

I beg your pardon, they were the pioneers and American-Indians.

Can you show me a Muslim signature in the United States of America's Constitution? The Declaration of Independence from England? The bill of Rights? I don't think so.

Maybe Muslims fought in the civil war, to free slaves in our country and to forever abolish slavery?

The answer is still no.

Not only did they not fight against the slavers, but until today, Muslims are the biggest slave traders in the world.

Your step-brother, a devout Muslim, still defends slavery, even if the Muslims of Arab descent refer to the black Muslims as PUG-NOSED SLAVES.

This speaks volumes as to how the Muslim world thinks of your family's rich Muslim heritage.

Where were the Muslims during the battles on human rights?

Non-present.

Where were the Muslims during the period of battles for women's rights.

Still non-present.

In fact, devout Muslims demand that women be submissive to men, and often in the Islamic culture, women are beaten and punished for not having worn the "hijab", or for having spoken to a man not related to the family.

Does it seem to you that Muslims are for women's rights?

Where were the Muslims during the Second World War?

They were allies of Adolf Hitler and the Nazis.

The Grand Mufti of Jerusalem, met in person with Hitler, and accepted his help in order to eliminate the Jews.

In the end Mr. Obama, where were the Muslims during 9-11 ?

Unless they were piloting the airplanes into the Twin Towers, the Pentagon and a field in Pennsylvania, killing around 3000 people on our own turf, they were celebrating in the Middle East and the rest of the world in general.

No one can question the videos taken within the Muslim world shown on CNN, Fox News, MSNBC and other stations, where the Muslims were celebrating the cowardly attacks.

Curiously, those moderate-Muslims that you kissed in Cairo the 4th of June, 2012, had remained in cold silence on that September 11, 2001.

To many Americans, their silence seemed like an approval for those cowardly acts.

Is this Mr. Obama, the rich Heritage that the Muslims have in America?

I beg your pardon, I had forgotten about the pirates in the Somalian coastline, also Muslims.

Now we can add the killings of American soldiers at Fort Hood, Texas, by a Muslim Major, also a doctor in psychiatry. He was supposed to help to heal our American soldiers, after Iraq and Afghanistan. It happened on the 5th of November, 2009.

This Mr. Obama, is the Muslim heritage in America.

P.S. To this we can add the bomb at the Boston marathon, and the decapitation of a British soldier on a London street.

Those misdeeds were not carried on by Buddhists, Catholics, Jews, followers of Confucius, but were performed by Muslims.

Every Canadian, American, Australian and British should read this e-mail and draw their own conclusions.

Muslim heritage in America? It is worth as much as my ass''.

ONLY FOR LAUGHS...MAYBE NOT

The English Coast Guard intercepts a dinghy in the English Channel, with four-Muslims on board. The captain asks where they were headed, "We are going to invade England" they answered.

"Is it only you four?", asks the captain.

"No, we are the last four, the rest are all in England", was the answer.

I received this e-mail during the first months of 2014. It is entitled "Agreements in order to meet Allah".

Let's forget the various speeches by Obama and let's read this powerful reply by an American Marine, war veteran, in regards to the decapitations of American journalists and a Scottish citizen, by the Isis assassins.

A veteran of the Marine Corps, sent a message via social media to the cowardly terrorists, Isis.

"Attack us and there will not be any piety for you. We will bring upon you the right hand of God and will destroy you''.

This strong message was written by Nick Powers, a war veteran who fought in Iraq, in answering to the assassins that decapitated American journalist, James Foley.

"To all of you, ignorant Islamic terrorists, from Mohammed which I constantly hear, and I see you kill innocent men, women and children, I smile softly.

Why do I smile at you?

Then let me explain to you a few things, stupid cowards that think you are so strong behind your videos of propaganda.

You are scaring a population that does not know how to fight back.

You are intimidating the weak.

You say that Islam is a peaceful religion, but when you start decapitating men, terrorizing innocent people, killing women and children, does that constitute peace?

Keep in mind what the Saddam's troops did when we arrived in the city, they gave up twice.

So, your ridiculous threats to come to America and to raise your black flag onto the White House, make me laugh more than you sadistic bastards can imagine.

In 2012 there were more than 21-milion war-veterans in the United States.

Imagine what that means.

Let me explain it to you.

It means that there are literally millions of veteran that are very upset and disgusted because you extremists idiots, do not act like human beings and do not want to give up your terroristic acts.

It is a simple thing to occupy an Islamic state, and if I remember correctly, it only took us four days in order to take Fallujah.

Better yet, we occupied the whole country in less than a month.

At this stage, with over 13-years of warfare on my back, how long do you think it will take to do it all over again?

I will leave the conclusion to you.

Do you really think that you can have even a minimum chance on American soil? Do you think it would be an intelligent thing for you to do?

Remember that in America we are armed to the teeth and I can assure you that in your case the Ginevra Convention would not have any value, and will not be applied in anyway.

If you attack us, there will be no piety.

We will bring the right hand of God upon you and destroy you.

Now the ball is in your hands, and remember that we are more than ready to send you to your 72 virgins and to meet your Mohammed.

If you think that what I have written is against Muslims in general, I suggest to you to look yourself in the mirror and ask yourselves a question, "Am I a terrorist?"

This letter is addressed to all the extremists and in all probability, if you are offended by it, then you are one as well.

E-MAIL FROM SEPTEMBER 2, 2014

This e-mail was written by an Australian citizen who contests the point of view of the politicians of the extreme left, on illegal immigration which evidently is afflicting even that far away country.

I am really annoyed by this crazy Hansen Young, who continues to criticize and attack Abbot, in regards to his methods in stopping illegal immigrants from coming to this country in great numbers, so I decided to send her this message.

The message is addressed to Senator Hanson Young, and was sent on the 14th of January, 2014, at exactly 17:05.
Subject: You and Islam
Like many normal people in our society, I have a big problem in guessing what planet you live on.
Your strident river of crap on the immigrants, is incredibly offensive for most Australians, and this is why you and your friends are able to get only 8 percent of votes on a national scale. Those are the crazies from the extreme left which you refer to.
Most of the illegal immigrants come from Muslim country, and if you had not noticed, 99 percent of terrorists come from those countries as well.
Every Muslim country in the Middle East is in total anarchy, and with a few exceptions, they are poor and violent and are not capable of governing themselves. Their vile Islamic religion, with its Jihad, and its Fatwas, vomits hate and terror all over the world, and whoever does not follow their doctrine is an infidel and should be killed. Naturally, Allah, is OK with all of this.
You, from the extreme left, besides all of this, you are at the forefront when it comes to helping them to come to this country.
Muslim immigration towards the civilized Western society, is an enormous drain on our welfare system and takes more money out than we would need to help our own needy citizens.
Most Muslims in the Western world are unemployed and unemployable, and they create stress and tension, squalor and a strong dependence on welfare.
In Denmark, the Muslim population is around 5 percent and it absorbs around 75 percent of welfare funds of that country.

The Muslims refuse to recognize the elected governments in the democratic countries, and are loyal only to their despicable Allah and the vile Sharia law, but they are happy to live at the expense of the Western country where they were able infiltrate.

I noticed that the Muslim community is the only ethnic group assigned a special constabulary. The Anti-Crime Team in Sydney, for the Middle East, with the aim of countering the widespread crime within the Muslim ghettos.

We have seen the two Muslim maniacs in London, who have killed a young decorated soldier with blows of an ax.

I assume that you would like to free them in order to try to rehabilitate them.

What do you have to say about the women that are considered only as goods by the Muslim men, and let's not talk about little girls that are forced into marriages with old men who they have never seen before.

Are you OK with that as well?

The immigrants that came here from Europe after the Second World War, were assimilated with the Australian society and contributed in creating what Australia is today.

Myself, a sixth-generation Australian, 71-years of age, married to a Dutch woman, very much admire all those people.

You keep on insisting on the discrimination factor, and on this point we could be in agreement, because as far as I'm concerned there is not enough of it.

The continuous killings, the drive by shootings in the western suburbs of Sydney, drug-dealing and organized crime, which have required the use of a police task force, the draining of our welfare system, they are all due to the Muslim immigrants.

And you still want more to come!

"I had received this e-mail on the 27th of August, 2014".

This is the lady that uses a slice of bacon as a bookmark when she's reading the Koran, and then rips the pages off and then burns them.
All this is on You Tube and you can watch the whole video by typing her name, Ann Barnhardt.
Unfortunately my comment can only be negative.
I cannot accept these actions which are light-years away from my way of thinking.
I don't think there is the necessity to commit those extreme acts which can offend the moderate Muslims, who we should have constructive dialogue with and projected into the future.
If someone were to make fun of the Gospel or the Bible which I'm a firm believer of, I would not be very happy about.
Do not do to others what you do not want done to yourself.

This is a good rule that everyone should follow.
Ann Barnhardt is a business broker dealing in beef and agricultural products.
American patriot and a traditional Catholic, has involuntarily become a counterrevolutionary.
She attacked Islam and they noticed.
Following is the death-threat to Ann Barnhardt.
"I will kill you when I will find you, don't think that I will not do it.
I know where you and your family live. All I need is a phone call in order to kill all of you".
Mufcadnan 123.
Here is Ann Barnhardt's answer.
"You will not have a need to find me, my address is 9175 Kornbrust Circle, Lone Tree, CO 80124.
Fortunately for you there are direct flights, Heathrow-Denver, daily.
This is what you have to do.
After you arrive in Denver and having gone through customs, take the airport shuttle to go rent a car.
When you are in the car get on Pena boulevard and onto I-225 South.
Proceed to the I-25 South, till Lincoln Avenue which is exit 193.
Go west on Lincoln Avenue, till the fourth traffic light, make a left going south, on Ridgegate Boulevard.
Keep on going south until you reach a circle and make a left on Kornbrust Drive and take the first right onto Kornbrust Circle. I live on 9175.
Do me only one favor, wear a bulletproof jacket.
I have some new ammunition that I would like to try and frankly, shooting you at short distance without any protection would be unsportsmanlike.

The fact that I'm probably 50 percent more intelligent than you are, gives you a tactical advantage. Anyway, you being a trembling coward, I understand that you will not be able to active any of your threats without losing control of your bowels and dirty your underpants when you're doing hyperventilation.
So why don't you contact the main mosque here in Denver, and see if there is another Muslim that would like to carry on those acts for you.
After all, this is what your perfect man, Mohammed, did.
You see, Mohammed, who was a miserable coward, used to send other people to fight for him.
He stayed backstage and let the ignorant and stupid believers like yourself, involved in his politics, to fight and die.
Then Mohammed would fornicate with the widows and daughters of the dead.
You should follow Mohammed's example.
Following I will write all contacts to the mosque.
Masjid Abu Bakr
Imam Karim Abu Zaid
2071 South Parker Road
Denver, CO 80231
Tel: 303 6969800
Email:denvermosque@yaho.com
I'm sure they will be happy to hear from you. Frankly, I'm very disappointed that not even one Muslim here in the States has tempted to rape me or decapitate me.
Maybe I was not too clear, so let me make things clear again now.
I will never submit, especially to Islam.
I will fight Islam with every fiber of my body, because Islam is a satanic devil.

If you are serious in saying that Islam will dominate America and the rest of the world, you will first have to step over my body.

You will have to kill me!

Good Luck.

You should know that if you or one of your Muslim friends succeed in killing me, the final crusade will begin 5-minutes after my death, so besides your genetic mental retardation, you will clearly understand the meaning of defeat.

Anyway, I will win!

DEO ADJUVANTE NON TIMENDUM

Ann Barnhardt.

This e-mail I received on the 5th of September, 2014, and evidently was sent by someone that does not love Muslims.

It's a little harsh and I will write it the same way as I received, even if I don't appreciate it nor share its meaning.

It talks about a sport where you usually jump off a bridge, a tower or a high-rise building, with an elastic harness attached to the body and as soon as you feel you're going to hit bottom, it pools you up again, bungee jumping.

It is a sport for fearless people and it is certainly not recommended to the weak hearted.

The publicity which you see written on the photo says:

Experience the jump in the open.

Only 35 pounds per jump.

Muslims go free, without harness attached to them.

New York City on Madison Ave!?
Date: Mon, 19 Jan 2015 19:40:03 -0800

PLEASE, JUST LOOK AT THE PICTURES BEFORE YOU READ THE BOTTOM COMMENTS CLOSEL!!

This is in NYC on Madison Ave - not France, Yemen, Kenya or the Middle East*

A Christian Nation cannot put up a Christmas scene of the baby Jesus in a public place, but the Muslims can stop normal traffic every friday afternoon by worshiping in the streets.... Something is happening in America & Canada and Australia that is reminiscent of what is happening in Europe. This is Political Correctness gone crazy.. Scary, isn't it?

Is there a message here???? Yes, there is, and they are laiming America & Canada for Allah. If we don't wake up soon, we are going to "politically correct" ourselves right out of our own country! It's time to make some changes people!

PLEASE SEND THIS TO EVERY Australian, Canadian & AMERICAN YOU KNOW!!!!

"For evil to flourish, all that is needed is for good people to do **nothing."**

The problem with Islam and Islamists in Europe exists, and it is very visible in cities such as Paris, London, Brussels, Amsterdam, Marseilles, Berlin, Liege and many other cities. To say that there is no problem would be a big lie, and to not do anything in order to stop this slow invasion but constant, would be a mortal sin.

This cannot be accepted by real Europeans, and all those who identify with our history and culture.

After many centuries Islam is succeeding in achieving its goal, to finally conquer the continent that for many centuries was the beacon of civilization.

Considering that militarily it would not be possible, but they have adopted the technique of peaceful invasion, for humanitarian reasons, health reasons, escaping from wars taking place in their countries and also to escape misery.

Welcoming is a Christian thing to do, but all those that receive our help have to respect our values and customs and should keep in mind that our multi millennia history was founded on Judeo Christian thought.

Whether one might like it or not.

To add on to all this is the fact that they procreate a lot more than Europeans, and that is very worrisome.

Time is on their side, and if we add the lack of a real vision in the Western world by the European governments , the inability to do so, means that in about 20-years, Islam's dream to occupy Europe will become a sad reality, and finally after Costantinopoli, there will also be the fall of Rome to Islam. The end of our liberty and our millenary civilization.

The author of this book basically assembled in a single volume all the e-mails that he had received within the last 3-years

He translated each one and transcribed into single volume.

Letters that most of the time have to do with Arabs and Muslims, and I received exactly the same way as you are able to read on this book.

You may notice that on this issue there is uneasiness in most western countries, because many realize that this problem is gripping without hope of freeing ourselves from all those issues which we have absolutely no need for.

Those that do not notice the problem are our politicians and the usual do-gooders, maybe because they think that in the near future they will be spared and given the white-glove treatment as gratitude for the enormous damage they caused in Europe, our liberties and our civilization, also to have had facilitated the infiltration of Muslims in our old and dear Europe.

Poor deluded people.

They do not realize that they will be the first to pay for the consequences of the debacle which they have helped create, with their indolence, cowardice, congenital inability to realize where the danger might be coming from.

Finito di stampare nel mese di Ottobre 2015
per conto di Youcanprint *Self-Publishing*

www.ingramcontent.com/pod-product-compliance
Lightning Source LLC
LaVergne TN
LVHW051122180726
843512LV00012B/905